The Discourse of Conflict and Crisis

Also available from Bloomsbury

Constructions of Migrant Integration in British Public Discourse,
by Sam Bennett
European Identities in Discourse, by Franco Zappettini
Language of Conflict, edited by Natalia Knoblock
The Language of Brexit, by Steve Buckledee
The Politics and Rhetoric of Commemoration, by Michael Billig
and Cristina Marinho

The Discourse of Conflict and Crisis
Poland's Political Rhetoric in the European Perspective

Piotr Cap

BLOOMSBURY ACADEMIC
LONDON • NEW YORK • OXFORD • NEW DELHI • SYDNEY

BLOOMSBURY ACADEMIC
Bloomsbury Publishing Plc
50 Bedford Square, London, WC1B 3DP, UK
1385 Broadway, New York, NY 10018, USA
29 Earlsfort Terrace, Dublin 2, Ireland

BLOOMSBURY, BLOOMSBURY ACADEMIC and the Diana logo are
trademarks of Bloomsbury Publishing Plc

First published in Great Britain 2022
This paperback edition published in 2023

Copyright © Piotr Cap, 2022

Piotr Cap has asserted his right under the Copyright, Designs and
Patents Act, 1988, to be identified as Author of this work.

For legal purposes the Acknowledgments on p. vii constitute an extension
of this copyright page.

Cover image: People in Krakow, Poland holding an EU flag and a Polish flag during
a protest against Supreme court reforms introduced by the government
© SOPA Images/ Getty Images

All rights reserved. No part of this publication may be reproduced or transmitted
in any form or by any means, electronic or mechanical, including photocopying,
recording, or any information storage or retrieval system, without prior
permission in writing from the publishers.

Bloomsbury Publishing Plc does not have any control over, or responsibility for, any
third-party websites referred to or in this book. All internet addresses given in this
book were correct at the time of going to press. The author and publisher regret any
inconvenience caused if addresses have changed or sites have ceased to exist,
but can accept no responsibility for any such changes.

A catalogue record for this book is available from the British Library.

LOC:
Names: Cap, Piotr, author.
Title: The discourse of conflict and crisis: Poland's political rhetoric
in the European perspective / Piotr Cap.
Description: London; New York: Bloomsbury Academic, 2021. |
Includes bibliographical references and index. |
Identifiers: LCCN 2021017359 (print) | LCCN 2021017360 (ebook) |
ISBN 9781350135635 (hardback) | ISBN 9781350135642 (ebook) |
ISBN 9781350135659 (epub)
Subjects: LCSH: Discourse analysis–Political aspects–Poland. |
Rhetoric–Political aspects–Poland. | Communication in
politics–Poland. | Politicians–Poland–Language. | Prawoi
Sprawiedliwos´c´ (Political party). | Right-wing
extremists–Poland–Language. | Right-wing extremists–Europe–Language.
Classification: LCC P302.77.C36 2021 (print) | LCC P302.77 (ebook) |
DDC 943.805/7–dc23
LC record available at https://lccn.loc.gov/2021017359
LC ebook record available at https://lccn.loc.gov/2021017360

ISBN: HB: 978-1-3501-3563-5
PB: 978-1-3502-7026-8
ePDF: 978-1-3501-3564-2
eBook: 978-1-3501-3565-9

Typeset by Deanta Global Publishing Services, Chennai, India

To find out more about our authors and books visit
www.bloomsbury.com and sign up for our newsletters.

Contents

List of Illustrations	vi
Introduction	1
1 "Do What I Say, Unless...": Political Leadership, Coercion, and Threat Construction	7
2 Polish Contexts: Threat-Based Communication and Crisis Management in Communist and Post-Communist Poland	35
3 Enemy at Home: "Total Opposition," "Post-Communist Elites," and "Keepers of the Round Table Order"	57
4 The "Worst Sort of Poles" Narrative	91
5 European Union and the Discourse of National Sovereignty	113
6 Oppressed by Neighbors: Germany, Russia, and Nord Stream 2	143
Concluding Remarks	155
Notes	159
Bibliography	165
Index	175

Illustrations

Figures

1.1	Discourse space in the DST model	22
1.2	DST representation of entities and events in Bill Clinton's address	24
1.3	Proximization in discourse space	30
3.1	Centralizing *now* for momentousness: 2 temporal proximization shifts (adapted from Cap 2013: 86)	77
3.2	Temporal proximization in text (11)	77
5.1	Axiological and spatiotemporal proximization in (15)	133

Table

3.1	The Most Frequent Lexical Items of the WAR Source Domain in the POLITICS/POLITICAL CONFLICT IS WAR Metaphor	67

Introduction

Context and Goals

October 2015 saw a major political change in Poland, marked by a landslide victory in parliamentary elections of the strongly conservative Law & Justice (L&J) party, which took over the legislative and executive powers after the eight-year rule of Civic Platform's liberal government. The resulting policy changes have been enormous, including rapid growth of state interventionism and central economic planning, constraints on the constitutional freedom and independence of the judiciary, as well as state control over the public media, among many others. No less radical have been L&J's changes in foreign policy, reflecting an essentially Eurosceptic disposition of the new government. The period of the past five years reveals a rich history of conflicts between Warsaw and Brussels, symbolized by EU's recent implementation of Article 7 of the Union treaty in response to the apparent democratic backsliding of state institutions in Poland. Since its coming to power in 2015 the L&J government has been defining anew Poland's position with respect to different critical issues surrounding Europe and the EU, such as the Eurozone crisis, populist movements, Brexit, climate change, or the migration crisis. Regarding the latter, L&J has vehemently refused to honor the EU refugee relocation agenda agreed on by the former government in spring 2015, arguing that it realizes a "German plan" at the expense of Poland's national interests.

While L&J's conflictual stance finds little understanding with most European partners, it enjoys high popularity on the home front, among Polish people. The party retained its parliamentary majority in the 2019 parliamentary elections, receiving the highest vote share by any party since Poland's return to democracy in 1989. The unfaltering support for L&J by its voters can be interpreted in a number of ways. From a sociopolitical perspective, the success of Law & Justice in Poland is believed to draw on the post-2000 rise of populist forces throughout Europe—the Alternative für Deutschland in Germany, the

National Front in France, Bepe Grillo's Movimento Cinque Stelle in Italy, Nigel Farage's United Kingdom Independence Party in Britain, the Freiheitliche Partei Österreichs in Austria, or Geert Wilders in the Netherlands (Cordell and Jajecznik 2015). According to Schmölz (2019), the example set by these forces exerted a substantial influence on the countries of Central Europe, leading to a certain—and apparently premature—"democracy fatigue." The latter would manifest itself in the departure from the rule of law as the foundation of liberal democracy as represented by European institutions in the name of the so-called sovereignty of the people, the repatriation of powers to the nation-states. Until 2015, the most extreme example of such a shift was arguably Hungary, where, "following the popular will," Prime Minister Victor Orban and his national-conservative FIDESZ party brought back to life judicial institutions and administrative regulations associated with the former communist dictatorship (Szilagyi and Bozoki 2015). These anti-democratic and anti-European changes in Hungary produced a massive sociopolitical divide, leading to the emergence of new radical rhetoric that inspired far-right groups and parties in other Central European states. After 2015, the L&J party and its leader Jarosław Kaczyński took over from FIDESZ the title of the largest and politically strongest far-right force in the region, enacting its leadership in Poland through its own special kind of populist rhetoric. Thus, L&J's success must be studied not only in sociological and political terms but also—and crucially—from a discursive standpoint.

This book explores the discursive features of L&J's leadership, explaining, in linguistic, pragmatic, and conceptual terms, the factors that underlie its win in the parliamentary elections of 2015 and, later, its continuing popularity leading to another election victory, in 2019. It defines the discursive mechanisms of social influence and coercion, such as conflict and crisis construction and threat generation, showing their role in legitimization of L&J's policies at home and abroad. The discussion focuses on a number of thematic and discourse-generic domains, such as parliamentary discourse in Poland, discourse of Poland's relations with the EU, as well as the rhetoric used by the L&J government in regard to issues involving Poland's two giant neighbors: Russia and Germany. Drawing upon analytical models of critical discourse studies and critical-cognitive pragmatics, it shows that the crisis, conflict, and threat elements in these domains activate public coercion and propaganda mechanisms that strengthen legitimization of L&J's leadership. Throughout the book, the analysis of Polish political discourse is intertwined with samples of right-wing discourses in other European countries (Hungary, Romania, Bulgaria, Italy, the UK, among others), demonstrating analogies with regard to the main themes (European integration, multiculturalism, immigration, welfare state), main rhetorical strategies (othering, enmification, fear appeals), and main actors that perform them. The aim of this combination is a panorama of Polish state-political discourse, coupled with a thought-provoking picture of ties and mutual dependencies among radical and populist right-wing discourse trends in contemporary Europe.

Overview of Chapters

The book is structured in six chapters. *Chapter 1* contains a general interdisciplinary discussion of the sociological, psychological, anthropological, and discursive underpinnings of political leadership, describing the key mechanisms and concepts, such as social coercion, threat-based communication, and policy legitimization. Drawing on evolutionary-psychological and persuasion theories of Bandura, Zimbardo and Leippe, Jowett and O'Donnell, and others, it argues for conflict and threat generation, and the ensuing crisis management, as central instruments of effective legitimization. It discusses the legitimization appeal of the bipolar *Us*-vs.-*Them* discourse representations, describing the coercive function of discursively construed, virtual threats from the symbolic *Them* entities. Finally, the chapter introduces relevant theories and models that provide the best tools to study the linguistic framework of these representations, such as deictic space theory, political metaphor, and proximization. *Chapter 2* places issues of social conflict, threat-based communication, and crisis management in the context of Poland's political situation after the Second World War, first during the communist years 1945–89 and then in the years following the establishment of the first democratic government in 1989. It demonstrates that notwithstanding some predictable differences related to changing historical context, Polish political leaders after the Second World War have been consistent in claiming legitimization of leadership based on discursively motivated social mobilization against a developing threat. The result is a firm entrenchment in the Polish public space of the *Us/Them* conceptual categories, and the tendency of consecutive leaders to define these categories according to current political interests. This mechanism is at its peak under the rule of the Law & Justice party, whose leaders not only take advantage of the aura of crisis caused by the *Us*-vs.-T*hem* conflict but in fact themselves provoke crisis situations, home and abroad, to propose "solutions" and thus legitimate their leadership.

Opening the empirical part of the book, *Chapter 3* focuses on Law & Justice's discourse on the home arena, specifically the discourse directed at the parliamentary opposition. This concerns, most of all, leaders of the Civic Platform (CP) party, which was in rule in the years 2007–15, losing to Law & Justice in the 2015 elections. The CP party is today the main oppositional force in the parliament and thus the main target of L&J's rhetoric. The chapter shows how L&J's discourse positions CP politicians at the remotest end of the *Us*/*Them* spectrum, construing them as unfaithful to "central Polish values" and "Poland's core interests." This involves a broad range of judgments and negative images: selling Polish property to foreign investors during the CP rule, inability to deal with growing unemployment and economic migration from Poland, promoting multiculturalism at the expense of Poland's cultural and religious heritage, incorporating non-Polish liberal values in family life, among others. The chapter demonstrates how these conceptualizations are enacted by linguistic-pragmatic means, particularly the STATE IS HOME, NATION IS BODY, and POLITICS IS WAR metaphors, as well as spatial, temporal, and axiological proximization strategies. The chapter concludes with an account of similar conceptual and linguistic strategies in other European discourses, such as the Northern League and 5 Star Movement's discourse during the 2018 government formation in Italy, and PM Victor Orban's discourse aimed at marginalizing his parliamentary and non-parliamentary opposition in Hungary. *Chapter 4* continues the analysis of L&J's home-front rhetoric, exploring its narrative of the "worst sort of Poles," a national out-group defined as such by L&J's leader Jarosław Kaczyński. The chapter demonstrates that Law & Justice includes in this out-group all those opposing the radically conservative ideology and values advocated by the ruling party. This makes the "worst sort" apply to different and heterogeneous groups of people: from feminist groups, to supporters of LGBT rights, to environmentalists demanding a decrease in coal production (a "national treasure" of Poland) to reduce air pollution. The conceptual othering of these groups involves several pragmalinguistic operations, such as deictic distancing, metaphorization, and, crucially, axiological proximization. It is argued in the chapter that L&J's "worst sort" narrative, albeit cynical and morally deplorable, reveals a number of analogies to other European state-level discourses, for instance the rhetoric of far-right politicians in Romania and Bulgaria.

In *Chapter 5* the focus moves from the home arena to the domain of international relations, specifically Poland's relations and status with(in) the EU. We have noted earlier that the first parliamentary term of the L&J rule (2015–19) reveals a long history of conflicts between Warsaw and Brussels, which are reflected in as well as created and then perpetuated by discourse. Chapter 5 explores the two principal areas in which these conflicts and mutual animosities arise. The first is the issue of migration and the clearly obstructionist stance of Law & Justice on EU immigration policies to handle the unprecedented migration crisis in Europe continuing since 2015. The second is L&J's overhaul of the judiciary in Poland, which has been criticized and formally opposed by EU institutions—such as the EU Commission and the European Parliament—eventually resulting in the implementation of Article 7 of the EU treaty. The discussion shows that the L&J government draws on these conflict domains to construct a specific kind of discourse, which can be termed the discourse of "national sovereignty." While such a discourse is developed in relation to international, mostly European, issues, its principal target group remains Polish political audience. To enhance legitimization of its political leadership L&J performs the sovereignty discourse by construing a range of political and ideological threats that extend over Poland seen, on the one hand, as an independent state and, on the other, as "a proud, sovereign nation." It is argued that in both conceptualizations L&J's discourse of national sovereignty reveals a staggering number of analogies to the discourse of Brexit, particularly the Eurosceptic rhetoric of Nigel Farage's UKIP party.

Finally, *Chapter 6* addresses issues of international economy, analyzing discursive aspects of relations between Poland and its two powerful neighbors: Germany and Russia. The chapter investigates L&J's discourse opposing the Nord Stream 2 (NS2) project, that is, construction of a gas pipeline enabling direct export of gas from Russia to Germany bypassing traditional transit countries, such as Poland, Ukraine, Belarus, Slovakia, and the Czech Republic. It shows how NS2 is construed by the L&J government as a gathering threat to the development of Poland's economy and, potentially, Poland's national security. It describes conceptual, pragmatic, and lexical tools that are used to present NS2 in terms of revival of imperialistic ambitions of European hegemons, a mind-set historically responsible for infamous political projects such as the 1939 Nazi–Soviet Molotov-Ribbentrop Pact. It explains the conceptual operations and mechanisms underlying L&J's NS2 rhetoric, whose function is to impose construals of geopolitical isolation and economic exclusion of Poland. Such construals involve specific metaphoric schemas, typically the STATE IS PERSON metaphor, as well as spatially perceived visions of external influence and impact. The chapter shows how these threatening visions contribute to the mobilization and consolidation of L&J's electorate in Poland, ensuring its unfaltering support for L&J's leadership. At the same time, it points to policy legitimization issues underlying criticism of the NS2 project in other Central and Eastern European countries, including Ukraine, Slovakia, and the Czech Republic.

1

"Do What I Say, Unless..."

Political Leadership, Coercion, and Threat Construction

The ability to generate an emotional response is the key to any leader's success and examples abound since antiquity. Moses got his people's undivided attention by putting the fear of a wrathful God in them. Winston Churchill appealed to the English sense of pride to rally spirits in the early, dark days of the Second World War. Martin Luther King, Jr., inspired the affection of millions by his own noble example of nonviolent leadership in the cause of civil rights for African-Americans. In 2003, George W. Bush invoked catastrophic visions of "another September 11" to win popular support for a preemptive strike on Iraq. And away from the world of politics we see, too, that business leaders, executives, and managers need to inspire emotions in order to persuade people to give their best. When it comes to social mobilization, emotions go a long way.

But does the nature of the emotion matter? Niccolo Machiavelli took on these questions centuries ago in the course of writing *The Prince*, famously advising at one point that "it is better to be feared than loved." Machiavelli was clear about which of the two emotions is likely to be more effective. Drawing on his sociopolitical study of ancient Rome, he conceded that there were indeed examples of men who led primarily "by love," and some were great leaders. But, according to him, those were still in minority. "Love is fickle," says Machiavelli in *The Prince*, and followers are likely to turn on their leader at the first sign that things are going badly. Fear is more reliable because it is "maintained by dread of punishment, which never fails" (Machiavelli 1532/2003: 46).

Five centuries after Machiavelli, most democratic leaders may not be followers of this stance in terms of their own image; nonetheless, fear continues to be the dominating emotion in modern political communication, even more so in the post-9/11 era of global anxiety and insecurity. It is not supposed to be fear *of* the leader anymore; it is, much rather, a fear that is inspired *by* the leader, and thus its source, object, or embodiment can be anyone and anything in the world—a looming storm, a wave of immigrants, or a terrorist attack. As found by *Time*'s Alex Altman, nearly 30% of the language used by Donald Trump in his 2016 election campaign included words and phrases depicting visions "in some way threatening" to American people (*Time*, February 9, 2017).

In this opening chapter we focus on the relations between fear and threat, political leadership, credibility, political discourse, and, crucially, discursive constructions of conflict and crisis. Eventually, we scrutinize scholarly theories and models that account for these relations. First, however, we need to address some general questions and issues from which these theories emerged. What are the core underpinnings, characteristics, and objectives of political leadership and political communication that make threat construction and fear generation so viable and widespread? And, conversely, what are the elements and features of threat-based discourse and crisis construction that help enact leadership in the best possible way?

1.1. Leadership and Communication: A Political Duo

One cannot speak about political leadership without discussing the concept of *politics* in the first place. Needless to say, there is no universal characterization, and it is not the business of this book to provide one. What we are interested in is, broadly speaking, what social aspirations, mechanisms, and goals make language and discourse the core elements of political behavior, that is, actions and practices geared toward realization of these goals. From this perspective, politics can be considered in two interrelated dimensions. On the one hand, politics involves a struggle for power, between "those who seek to assert and maintain their power and those who seek to resist it" (Chilton 2004: 3). On the other hand, politics can be seen as cooperation, a set of practices designed to resolve various clashes of interest that arise in a society—over money, social influence, freedom, and the like. In both of these dimensions, doing politics means contributing to a collection of voices on top issues of social order, economy, law, education, and other areas of public interest and participation. On this broad view, politics is, in the words of Habermas (1981), about "sharing visions"; it has the continual goal of maximizing the number of common conceptions of current reality, as well as its future developments. Emerging from the aforementioned view is the notion of political leadership: the ability to ensure public approval of a joint course of action prescribed by the leader in order to realize the invoked vision (Cap 2017).

Soliciting public acceptance for common action entails that political leader must reconcile the existing differences of opinion through discussion and persuasion. This makes politics rely heavily on the art of *communication*; most crucially, the ability to present future visions as beneficial to audience, assuming that the actions and policies proposed by the leader are unequivocally approved and followed. Political communication is essentially bipolar and coercive, discursively placing the leader, her audience, and all allies in a "home camp" (a geopolitical "*Us*"), and thus excluding, marginalizing, and stigmatizing those in opposition to the home camp (a geopolitical "*Them*") (we will take an in-depth look at this critical distinction in the next section). Coercion can be exercised not only by the speaker's (leader's) own discourse but also through the control of others' discourse—that is, through various kinds and degrees of censorship and access control. The latter include the structure and management of the media, the arena where much political communication takes place (Fetzer and Lauerbach 2007), either directly or in a recontextualized form (Cap and Okulska 2013). Importantly, it appears that the coercive element in political communication may involve the strategic stimulation of affect (Chilton 2014). Although the precise links are still under-researched, there seem to exist connections between meaning structures produced via discourse; in other words, certain kinds of text can stimulate certain hormones and the effect may be automatic (Hart 2014).

Coercion strategies naturally entail *legitimization*, a complex concept and a complex practice involving a linguistic enactment of the speaker's right to be listened to and obeyed (Chilton 2004; Cap 2008). As noted by Chilton (2004), the claim to rightness is grounded in the speaker's implicit claim to inhabit a particular social role and to possess a particular authority (Martin and Wodak 2003). The possession of authority provides rationale for listing reasons to be obeyed. This involves a symbolic assignment of different values to different discourse parties (such as *Us* and *Them* opposites), a firm assertion of audience's wants and needs in the moment of crisis, and, crucially, the construction of charismatic leadership needed to handle the crisis situation (Huntington 2004; Cap 2017). All these practices are components of successful legitimization, whose central objective is a broad social mobilization around a common goal. Legitimization is thus a universal weapon: it can be "a good means to a good end," as well as "a bad means to a bad end" (Cap 2017: 3; Hartman 2002).

In political communication, legitimization is often accompanied by *delegitimization* (Chilton 2004; Cap 2006, 2017), the strategy of presenting others (e.g., foreigners, "enemies within," political opposition, institutional adversaries) as "bad" and potentially hostile. Delegitimization involves the use of ideas of difference and geopolitical as well as ideological and cultural boundaries. In that sense it partakes, together with legitimization, in defining and positioning of the *Us* and *Them* camps at opposite ends of a scale. Pragmatically, delegitimization can manifest itself in acts of negative *Them*-presentation, acts of blaming, scapegoating, marginalizing, excluding, attacking the moral character of an individual or a group, or attacking the rationality and sanity of the other. The extreme is to deny the humanness of the other—a strategy adopted, for example, in the anti-Semitic propaganda in the Nazi Germany. In general, delegitimization strategies are widely present in state interventionist discourses (Oddo 2018), where leaders use them to foster legitimization of the proposed preventive or reactionary policies (Oddo 2018; Koller et al. 2019). These days such manifestations of delegitimization are notably salient in the anti-terrorist and anti-immigration rhetoric (Cap 2017; Oddo 2018), or as elements of complex national discourses such as Brexit discourse (Koller et al. 2019).

The concepts and manifestations of coercion, legitimization, and delegitimization, and their mutual relations in which they enter in discourse, endorse the conception of political leadership and political communication as inextricably intertwined. If politics is, as we have observed, about "sharing visions" (Habermas 1981), then language and communication are powerful tools whereby a political speaker is able to convince her audience to a particular course of action regardless of where and when it takes place. This is because we as humans have the ability to not only represent, but also, and crucially, *meta-represent*, things (Sperber 2000). In other words, human communication is a system that, among other things, includes symbols that are detached from their direct referents (Hockett 1960). Thus, we can communicate about things not only present but equally past, future, possible and impossible, permissible, and impermissible—from the point of view of the communicator(s) (Gardenfors 2002; Chilton 2004). This ability emerges as critical in political discourse, which often relies on analogy or other spatial and temporal projections and shifts for successful legitimization of future action.

1.2. *Us* and *Them* or *Them* vs. *Us*? The Politics of Fear Dichotomies

The relations between coercion, legitimization, and delegitimization and the social goals served by these strategies and practices reflect a specific nature of political communication. In general, political communication operates *indexically*, with a view to enacting sociopolitical affiliations and distinctions. These distinctions are embedded in mental representations that political leaders continually define, enforce, negotiate, and redefine through language, to maximize the number of the promoted visions. As noted by Hockett (1960), the key *Us*-and-*Them* distinction is probably the result of anthropological developments, such as the two-tier organization of human sociopolitical perception. On the one hand, people possess a mental ability to structure their cognitive experience ("looking at" the world) in terms of dichotomous representations of good and evil, right and wrong, acceptable and unacceptable. On the other hand, they possess a strictly linguistic ability to evoke or reinforce these dichotomous, bipolar representations in accordance with their social goals (Hockett 1960; Chilton 2004). The central goal involves, let us repeat, getting others to share a common view on what is good/evil, right/wrong, acceptable/unacceptable, and so on, and, consequently, how to secure the "right," "good," "useful," "just," "acceptable," against a possible intrusion, in the life of a society, of the "wrong," "evil," "harmful," and so on. Thus, political communication nearly always presupposes *distance* between the *Us* party (the home group and its leader or leaders) and the *Them* party (the possible "intruder"). Recent intercultural discourse research (Cap 2013, 2017; Abdi and Basarati 2018) demonstrates that perception of the *Us* camp by its members has a direct and universal influence on speaker's discourse. The more specific the *Us* party and the more consequential or broader the goals (as in, e.g., state-level discourse), the clearer the marking of the distance through linguistic means. The "good" and "right" are thus construed and lexicalized as "close to *Us*," and the "wrong" and "evil" as "remote to *Us*" (Cap 2017; Abdi and Basarati 2018).

The possibility to use discourse to control the perceived distance between *Us* and *Them* is an essential asset in political communication, especially in reactionary political projects that require swift social response and mobilization to face the emerging conflict (Dunmire 2011). The clearer the outlines of the conflict and the bigger the threat involved, the quicker, normally, the response. As found by anthropological and sociopsychological research, the success of threat-based communication nearly always relies on conceptualization of consequences of the conflict or crisis as personal and close (Zimbardo and Leippe 1991; Bandura 1986). Public audiences are generally reluctant to accept and legitimate radical policies, unless they are proposed in response to developments posing direct danger to specific groups or individuals. The danger can be physical and involving an apparent threat to life (as in state discourses of military intervention such as war-on-terror) or, as often happens, it can affect the well-being of social structures or interests of individual people. Thus, the construal of imminent and gathering threat from the antagonistic *Them* camp paves the way for legitimization of reactionary, preventive, as well as preemptive measures in a vast number of public discourses at various levels of state organization. These include public health, environment, technology, education, and many other domains (Cap 2017).

The construction of the *Us*-and-*Them* opposition and conflict generating the aura of threat and fear often involves activation of analogical reasoning (Bartha 2010), which, as we observed, is a distinctive feature of human communication and its capacity for meta-representation. Analogy is a powerful instrument of social coercion and legitimization, playing a major role in construal of the *Them* party and its potential for threatening action. Technically, it establishes a retrospective link between the current crisis situation and a past situation in which the threat materialized as a result of negligence (Cap 2017). As such, it delivers a prompt for immediate (and legitimate) preemptive response. This mechanism—swift legitimization by analogy—can be observed in multiple instances of contemporary political communication, particularly in interventionist discourses. Silberstein (2004) and Oddo (2018) note that much of the global anti-terrorist rhetoric, especially the rhetoric developed after the 9/11 attacks, includes claims of "inaction" following the UN anti-terrorist resolutions of the 1990s. These claims are used by political leaders to form narrative scenarios of "lessons from the past" and "for the future," sanctioning prompt response (often involving military measures) in the current crisis situation. For example, in November 2015 the then-president of France Francois Hollande announced French air operation on the city of Raqqa in an attempt to destroy the ISIS headquarters in Syria (Cap 2017: 9). In the way of rhetorical preparation, he constructed a scenario in which the earlier coalition-led policies were deemed "inadequate" and in fact responsible for increased terrorist activity of the Islamic State.

As can be seen from the aforementioned outline, the "*Us* and *Them*" distinction in political communication often turns into a "*Them* vs. *Us*" distinction, a strategic way in which the antagonistic party is positioned by the political leader/speaker as apparently remote yet ready to encroach on the home territory of the speaker and her audience. This construal serves as a coercive prerequisite for legitimization of preventive response. We can consider such mechanism *politics of fear dichotomies*, that is, management of a network of discursive patterns involving the use of analogy as well as other means (e.g., credibility ploys, which we discuss in the next section) to construct vision of a threatening adversary to evoke crisis and fear. Naturally, instilling the aura of crisis and fear requires the speaker's dichotomies to be communicated in large numbers and to surface widely in the public domain (Marlin 2013). This is to say, in other words, that the speaker must be able to meet conditions for efficient sociopolitical propaganda (Jowett and O'Donnell 2015).

Expertise in performing propaganda is an essential element of political leadership. This is because propaganda and its discursive techniques induce *recontextualization*, prompting new audiences "to further spread the message without altering or undermining it" (Oddo 2018: 3). As a consequence of recontextualization all the original content of the message—from pragmatically neutral to legitimizing, delegitimizing, coercive, or otherwise manipulative—becomes perpetuated by and among masses of people. Ideological and geopolitical affiliations and distinctions, such as *Us* and *Them*, are particularly keen to travel through such propagandistic channels, as they involve deeply embedded evolutionary characteristics that can readily be addressed. The same holds, generally, for most potentially fearful representations. Of course, there is still some work for the leader/speaker to do to induce favorable uptake and recontextualization. In principle, the original message must be, as Urban (1996: 23) puts it, "detachable" and "shareable"; the text carrying it must be extractable from larger discourse and easily entextualizable in a new piece of text. Apparently, argues Urban, "some kinds of text and discourse are intrinsically more shareable than others" (: 24). For instance, messages involving rhetorical devices such as ideologically charged words, parallelism, reiteration, and metaphor make recontextualization and sharing more likely. Another feature of shareable texts is what Ridolfo and De Voss (2009) call their "rhetorical velocity," that is how and to what extent the recontextualized information could be useful not only for the original speaker (political leader), but also for those parties which redistribute it (for instance the media). Competent political leaders will thus try to anticipate a future text trajectory favorable to them, maximizing the possibility that others will recompose and circulate their discourse in their own interest as well. Needless to say, construals of a fearful adversary, a potent *Them* entity, tend to be quite appealing to many such recomposers. Specifically, TV news producers value discourse that is pithy, sensational, and striking, such as sound bites that contain intense evaluation and highlight conflict and drama (Cramer 2013).

An important feature of propaganda that makes it a workable tool in instilling a sense of threat from the antagonist involves the perceived veracity of communication. In short, propaganda can manipulate without necessarily being false. Oddo (2018: 4) observes that in the course of message circulation, its recipients may be manipulated because one truth salient in the message "becomes so dominant that other relevant truths are overwhelmed and obscured." In other words, propaganda discourse may be accurate, factual, and logical—yet still hegemonic and therefore coercive. Oddo (2018) provides a telling example from the 2002–03 rhetoric of the Persian Gulf crisis. Back in the 1980s, Iraqi president Saddam Hussein used illegal chemical weapons in a war against Iran. In 2002 and early 2003 this fact was repeated often by the US government as it argued for removing Saddam from power. But, as Oddo (2018) shows, such "truthful" assertions can still be misleading. Saddam indeed used chemical weapons but only with American help: the US government had not only supplied such weapons but had even helped Iraq locate Iranian targets (Borger 2002).

1.3. Conflict Construction and Credibility

As we have seen, politics of fear dichotomies and its discursive manifestations play a major role in the enactment of strong leadership, necessary to manage the envisaged crisis. Public perception of crisis grows as the established "*Us and Them*" distinction gradually turns into a more dynamic "*Them* vs. *Us*" power confrontation, constituting a direct threat to members of the home camp. The aura of such an ominous confrontation reveals, according to conflict research, several leadership and legitimization benefits. Most notably, it helps maintain integrity, solidarity, and unification of the leader's home group (Simmel 1955; Królikowska 2015). In addition, it helps define (and potentially redefine, if necessary) the boundaries between the parties involved and thus centralize authority (Coser 1975). The success in earning these benefits depends, however, on the leader's/speaker's ability to follow a number of strategies for political as well as personal credibility (Królikowska 2015). Some of these strategies stem from findings of sociopsychological and political studies, and others are either their discourse oriented elaborations or independent proposals arising from the field of linguistics.

In the area of social psychology, there are two relevant theories. First, the *latitude of acceptance theory* (Sherif and Hovland 1961; Jowett and O'Donnell 2015) maintains that the best credibility effects can be expected if the speaker produces her message in line with the psychological, social, political, cultural, or religious predispositions of the audience (Jowett and O'Donnell 2015). However, since full compliance is almost never possible, it is essential that the new message be at least tentatively or partly acceptable—then, its acceptability and the speaker's credibility are going to increase over time. This last finding lies at the heart of another psychological model, known as *consistency theory* (Festinger 1957; Aronson 1969). Festinger (1957) observes that the increase in credibility over time can be attributed to human drive toward *consistency in belief* and *homeostasis*, a state of mental stability. Namely, in the long run, people find it difficult to tolerate dissonance in their judgments, especially with regard to the same issue or topic. Thus, if there is a new message that could produce such a conflict, people try to see any positive aspects of it—so they can still accept it in accordance with their preexistent ideological or moral groundwork. Naturally, for this mechanism to work "the message must not be entirely rejectable from the very start" (Cap 2017: 10) and at least some parts of it must be congruent with audience's predispositions. History of political communication demonstrates that human consistency in belief is among the most addressed sociopsychological mechanisms and top political speakers, such as state leaders, indeed take heed of it. In his comprehensive account of Franklin D. Roosevelt's (FDR) rhetoric, Hunt (2003) discusses the president's multiple appeals to ideological consistency in judging his proposal for "redistribution of workforce population" in an attempt to speed up industrialization of hitherto rural areas of the country. As noted by Hunt (2003), FDR's argument would frequently include flashbacks of people's mobility in early America, defining it in terms of an inherent virtue of the nation—"a firm commitment to the continual pursuit of better life for all American citizens" (: 377–8). These images served to remind Americans of their legacy and moral obligations, thus helping legitimization of the current mobility plan.

Issues of credibility in political communication have also been amply investigated in anthropological and evolutionary research, producing seminal interdisciplinary theories and concepts, such as *cheater detection module* (Cosmides 1989; Sperber 2000). Cheater detection module was originally (Axelrod 1984; Cosmides 1989) proposed as a logico-rhetorical device that evolved in human cognition to resist acts of deception, through the checking of speaker's coherence in communication. In later research this basic characterization underwent several modifications. As a result, cheater detection module is seen today not only as a defense mechanism on the part of the addressee, but also, and crucially, as a mighty persuasion tool available for the speaker. In Dan Sperber's (2000: 136–7) words, while for the addressee the module provides "a means to filter communicated information," for the speaker it offers "a means to penetrate the filters of others." In this communicative "arms race," as Sperber calls it, political speakers make strategic displays of discourse coherence to neutralize the operation of the cheater detection module in the audience so as to maximize credibility and thus strengthen their leadership (Sperber 2000). Examples of coherence displays include the ample use of deictic markers and clausal connectors ("and," "or," "since," etc.), giving an impression of order, logic, and rationality (Hart 2010). An interesting empirical analysis of lexical ploys used in such displays is Karv's (2012) study of plenary debates in the European Parliament, endorsing most of Sperber's findings.

Over years, the sociopsychological, anthropological, and cognitive-evolutionary accounts of credibility have been coexistent, more or less conspicuously, with a number of linguistically oriented studies. As evidenced by Cap (2017: 11), in linguistics (and language philosophy generally) issues of credibility have often surfaced in theories of pragmatics, such as *speech act theory* (e.g. Searle 1979) and the theory of *conversational implicature* (Grice 1975). In the former, credibility has been approached in terms of an illocutionary-perlocutionary force, or "potential" (Searle 1979), of certain acts, usually assertions. This track has been followed by Jary (2010), who claims that assertion acts are helpful in establishing credibility due to some intrinsic content–related features and default pragmatic functions. These are, for example, predication of facts, reference to objective truths, or expression of popular beliefs in line with the predispositions of the addressee. According to Jary (2010), assertions seldom perform these jobs individually; they tend to occur in textual or discursive sequences that collectively build up the credibility needed to pursue actions and policies. Since those actions or policies are usually communicated through directive acts constituting a potential source of dispute or controversy, assertions contribute an important preemptive element. Namely, they set up a firm link between the directive, its rationale, and the logic or truth expressed in the assertion. In so doing, they sanction a potentially controversial future act by the speaker based on the hitherto established trust and acceptance from her addressee. A powerful example of such a mechanism in political communication comes from President John F. Kennedy:

> [Today], the same revolutionary beliefs for which our forebears fought are still at issue around the globe—the belief that the rights of man come not from the generosity of the state, but from the hand of God. We dare not forget today that we are the heirs of that first revolution. Let the word go forth from this time and place, to friend and foe alike, that the torch has been passed to a new generation of Americans [. . .] proud of our ancient heritage—and unwilling to witness or permit the slow undoing of those human rights to which this Nation has always been committed, and to which we are committed today at home and around the world. (Inaugural Address of John F. Kennedy, January 20, 1961)

In the opening assertion part, Kennedy glorifies the American legacy, expressing dedication to values shared by a vast majority of his compatriots. Having earned the initial acceptance and credibility, he transposes these values into the domain of (controversial) foreign policies, which are communicated in an indirect directive ("unwilling to witness or permit"). In so doing, he implicitly steers the addressee toward considering these policies (involving a potential military intervention) in terms of enactment of American heritage. From the perspective of argumentation theory (Van Eemeren and Grootendorst 2004), such a communicative sequence represents *modus ponens*, a syllogistic strategy of persuasion involving recognition of truth in the consequent (the directive part) based on the truthfulness of the antecedent (the assertion part).

As was mentioned, another linguistic-pragmatic concept bound up with credibility is conversational implicature (henceforth: implicature; Grice 1975; Levinson 2000), which plays a key role in upholding policy legitimization and maintaining leadership over time. Implicature has the power to launch a vast spectrum of possible meanings inferred differently by different addressees in accordance with their individual expectations, wants, and needs. Since any such inference can be "canceled" by the speaker in a prospective discourse (e.g., by adding more content; Horn 2004), implicature strengthens legitimization and leadership not only in the present reality but also in the future, "updated" reality. Specifically, it redefines and re-legitimizes actions for the new context and new predispositions or priorities of the addressee. The process where the political speaker monitors the current needs of the addressee, enforcing or canceling inferences accordingly, reflects operation of the cheater detection module. Namely, the speaker is constantly sensitive to whether her original message, text, and legitimization pattern are still coherent and "work for" the addressee, or maybe there is already a need to alter the rhetoric. To see a particularly lucid example of such a forced transition, let us return to the context of the Gulf crisis, specifically the American military intervention in Iraq in March 2003. The rationale for that intervention was, as we know, the alleged possession of weapons of mass destruction (WMD) by Saddam Hussein. That allegation, perpetuated by the Bush administration and most of the American media, served as the cornerstone of the US pro-war rhetoric for the first eight months of the conflict (Oddo 2018). But when in October 2003 the UN inspections revealed no presence of WMD in Iraq, the Bush government had to find a new legitimization premise for the Iraq war. The idea was, of course, that the new premise would not make nonsense or otherwise detract from the truth of the original premise. Consequently, the phrase "programs for WMD" was coined at the end of 2003, replacing the original "WMD" phrase. The function of the new phrase was to induce two seemingly disparate, yet equally valid and acceptable, inferences at the same time. One would see WMD as a "product" and thus a direct threat in accordance with the original premise, and the other would see it as a mere "conception" (Silberstein 2004). Serving such a dyadic function until the end of the war, "programs for WMD" became a classic example of how implicature can contribute to political discourse in the way of rhetorical flexibility and efficiency (Cap 2017).

We should finally note that the pragmatic findings on credibility are endorsed by a number of studies in text and corpus linguistics, especially the research in the evidential underpinnings of communicative acts (spoken and written), such as assertions. For example, Bednarek (2006) identifies four specified bases of knowledge used as evidence in the British newspaper reporting of transnational conflicts and crises: (i) perception, (ii) general knowledge, (iii) proof, and (iv) obviousness. These underlying bases of knowledge add to the credibility of the respective assertions in different ways, drawing on different types of evidence. *Perception* provides directly attested sensory evidence, whose existence is indicated in discourse by phrases such as "it appears that" or "visibly." The evidence is thus construed as acquired directly via visual perception or as something made available to see. Evidence from *General Knowledge* is "marked as based on what is regarded as part of the communal epistemic background" (Bednarek 2006: 640) and the most typical markers are "widely held [view(s), opinion(s)]" and "everybody knows (it/that)." Hart (2010) observes that this pattern of credibility-building reflects what Van Leeuwen and Wodak (1999) call "conformity authorization," involving the *ad populum* fallacy that something is true if everyone believes it. Evidence from the *Proof* base is expressed by lexical markers such as "research," "results," or "statistics," which "show," "indicate," or "reveal" facts. Lastly, *Obviousness* provides evidence from the so-called facts of life—self-evident claims containing phrases such as "obviously" or "clearly." Altogether, the four bases of knowledge and their respective markers often partake in what Groom (2000) calls *source-tagging*. He defines source-tagging as a judgment attribution strategy, involving the use of an authoritative source or voice to communicate "sensitive, controversial or otherwise difficult information" (Groom 2000: 24).

1.4. Analytical Models: DST, Political Metaphor, and Proximization

The argument so far has been only a synthetic account of the conceptual, theoretical, and, eventually, analytical issues of political leadership and political communication. Emerging from this account is a number of essential features and inherent mechanisms of political communication that must be considered and addressed in research work. The following list is an attempt to group together the most important and consequential characteristics:

1. Political communication operates indexically. It uses linguistic and discursive means to define and enact sociopolitical affiliations and distinctions.
2. The principal distinction in political communication is enacted by the *Us* vs. *Them* dichotomy. The "*Us*" and "*Them*" mark, respectively, the speaker/leader and her sociopolitical in-group, and the remote and potentially threatening out-group.
3. The "remoteness" of the sociopolitical out-group is defined in physical, geopolitical, as well as ideological terms.
4. Political communication sets and controls the conceptual distance between the *Us* and *Them* camps in the interest of social coercion and threat generation. As the distance shrinks, the outlines of the threat grow.
5. The threat element of political communication plays a crucial role in the enactment of strong, legitimate leadership. The discursive construction of crisis increases in-group solidarity and induces support from the home camp.
6. Political communication makes ample use of propagandistic discursive strategies, such as text sharing and recontextualization, to reach the broadest audience possible and maximize the support.
7. To earn credibility for policy legitimization and support, political communication targets specific sociopsychological predispositions of the audience, such as consistency in belief and homeostasis.

These seven points are just as much observations on the nature of political communication per se, as a list of challenging preconditions for virtually all theories and models in political discourse analysis (PDA), including, of course, models of crisis construction and threat-based communication. Fortunately, recent advances in PDA, originating mostly in the rapidly expanding area of critical discourse studies (CDS), seem to provide enough tools to meet such a challenge. These days, most accounts of the field (Hart and Cap 2014; Van Dijk 2015; Flowerdew and Richardson 2018) agree that the greatest explanatory potential lies at the intersection of cognitive-scientific and functional approaches, especially cognitive linguistics and pragmatics, and a number of more nuanced approaches to discourse study informed by various qualitative and quantitative methodologies (for instance cognitive corpus linguistics; Arppe et al. 2010). The interaction between all these schools and perspectives has given rise to what Hart (2018) calls the "cognitive-linguistic CDS"—an eclectic critical approach incorporating vast amounts of work on spatial cognition and conceptualization (Fauconnier and Turner 2002; Levinson 2003; Evans and Chilton 2010) into interdisciplinary studies of pragmatically motivated construals of meaning within different discourse domains. As noted by Hart (2018), the cognitive-linguistic CDS offers a disciplined theoretical view of the conceptual import of pragmatic and linguistic choices identified as potentially ideological. In doing so, it affords an excellent lens on the many persuasive, manipulative, and coercive properties of discourse.

Most crucially, however, the cognitive-linguistic CDS offers workable methodologies and tools to deal with issues of conflict, coercion, and threat construction in political discourse, including the state-level discourse of political leaders. While the particular research models within the cognitive-linguistic CDS reveal differences in empirical focus, they all agree on the fundamental conceptual premises. First, they take the *Us*-and-*Them* distinction as the default cognitive representation enacted in sociopolitical communication. Second, they recognize the *Us*-vs.-*Them* (and *Them*-vs.-*Us*) opposition as the principal conceptual arrangement in threat and crisis generation. Third, they acknowledge the role of the threat element in social coercion and, potentially, legitimization of political leadership. In what follows, we review three such models, which possess arguably the largest analytical depth and offer the greatest explanatory power.

1.4.1. Discourse Space Theory

Proposed and developed by Paul Chilton (2004, 2005, 2010, 2011, 2014), discourse space theory (DST) has been a pioneer among the cognitive-critical models of political discourse (and discourse in general), inspiring several other theories, including the ones we discuss in the next two sections. The central claim of DST is that in performing discourse we open up a particular kind of mental space in which the "world" described in the discourse is conceptually represented. This discourse space consists of three intersecting axes around which the discourse world is constructed by positioning ideational elements in the text in relations with one another as well as with the speaker inside this space. Each of these axes represents a scale of relative "distance" from a deictic center. The three axes are a spatial axis (S), a temporal axis (T), and a modal axis (M). In his recent overviews of DST, Hart (2014, 2018) observes that the modal axis is in fact an evaluative axis engaged in an epistemic (E_e) as well as axiological (E_a) aspect. The deictic center represents the speaker's (and her audience's) current point of view in the social, temporal, epistemic, and axiological space. All other entities and processes "exist" in positions defined by their coordinates on the S, T, and M axes. In recognizing these entities and processes as occupying or changing a particular position in the three-dimensional zone extending from the deictic center, we conceptualize the ongoing kaleidoscope of ontological configurations activated in discourse Figure 1.1.

DST is thus an essentially deictic model,[1] engaged in coding spatial, temporal, and modal-evaluative distance relative to the speaker's situational

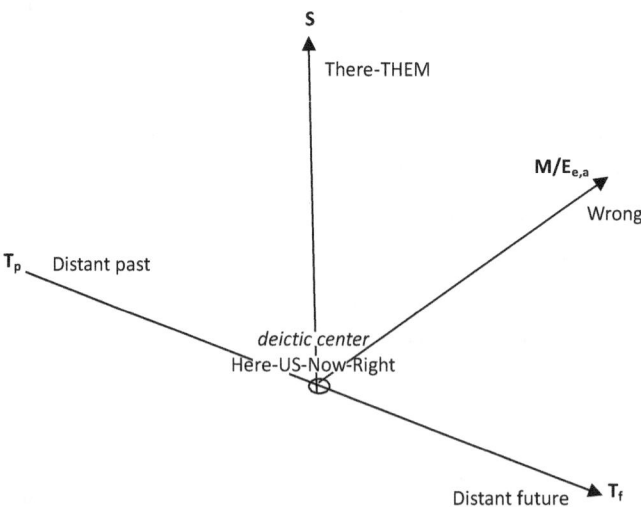

Figure 1.1 Discourse space in the DST model.

coordinates at the moment of utterance. This is reflected most obviously in oppositions arising from the linguistic use of adverbs (such as "here" vs. "there," "now" vs. "then"), demonstratives ("this" vs. "that"), and personal pronouns ("us" vs. "them"). However, in DST the notion of deixis is often decoupled from immediate situational dependencies and is extended to cover the speaker's broader conceptualization of what counts as "we," "here," "now," or "acceptable" in sociopolitical terms. Within the arena of geopolitics this involves representing such ideas and concepts as national identities, collective memories, historical moments or time periods, political systems, religious beliefs, or moral truths. In one of his first exposes of DST, Chilton (2004) demonstrates how his three-dimensional explanatory framework can be used to account for interventionist legitimization discourse produced in the context of a major geopolitical conflict. In his study, Chilton (2004: 142–8) engages with the American discourse of the Kosovo war, analyzing a series of excerpts from the 1999 speeches by President Bill Clinton. The most comprehensive analysis involves Clinton's CNN address of March 24, in which an attempt is made to alert the American and international audience to the gravity of the situation, thus sanctioning a prospective military intervention. Chilton (2014: 142–3) works with the following text:

> Ending this tragedy is a moral imperative. It is also important to America's national interest. Take a look at this map. Kosovo is a small place, but it sits on a major fault line between Europe, Asia and the Middle East, at the meeting place of Islam and both the Western and Orthodox branches of Christianity. To the south are our allies, Greece and Turkey; to the north, our new democratic allies in Central Europe. And all around Kosovo there are other small countries, struggling with their own economic and political challenges—countries that could be overwhelmed by a large, new wave of refugees from Kosovo. All the ingredients for a major war are there: ancient grievances, struggling democracies, and in the center of it all a dictator in Serbia who has done nothing since the Cold War ended but start new wars and pour gasoline on the flames of ethnic and religious division. Sarajevo, the capital of neighboring Bosnia, is where World War I began. World War II and the Holocaust engulfed this region. In both wars Europe was slow to recognize the dangers, and the United States waited even longer to enter the conflicts. Just imagine if leaders back then had acted wisely and early enough, how many lives could have been saved, how many Americans would not have had to die. We learned some of the same lessons in Bosnia

just a few years ago. The world did not act early enough to stop that war, either.

The meaning of this text can be defined, argues Chilton, in terms of the following 3D representation:

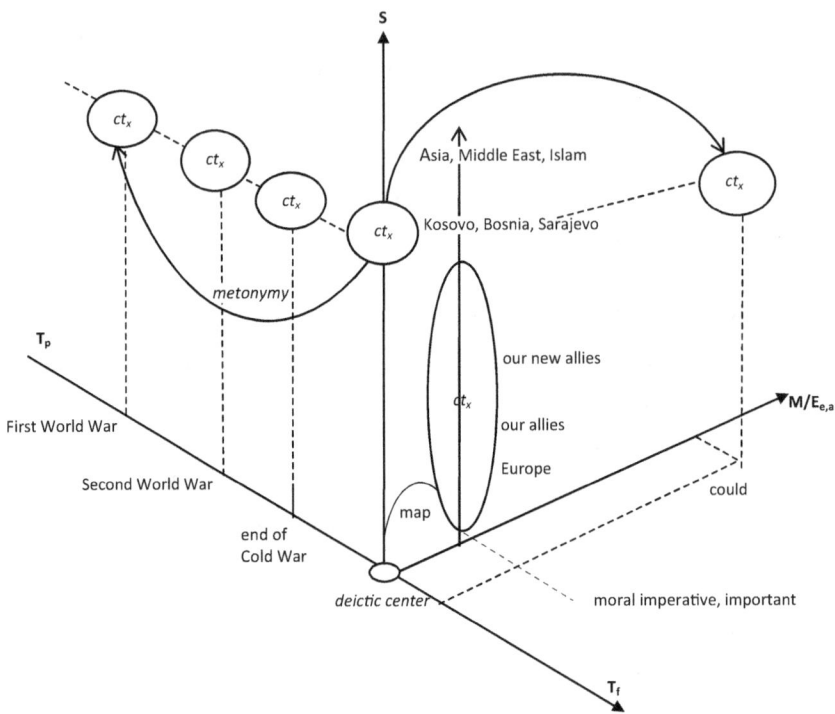

Figure 1.2 DST representation of entities and events in Bill Clinton's address.

To elucidate Chilton's methodology (rather than providing a meta-analysis), Figure 1.2 has been slightly edited from the original. In the original version, the oval spaces include numbers indicating sentences in the Kosovo text. Chilton's idea is to demonstrate how (and which) linguistic expressions in the text partake in the construals of meaning involving combination of spatial, temporal, as well as evaluative awareness and reasoning. Defining meanings in terms of spatiotemporal and evaluative coordinates is, however, a universal property of the model and thus in Figure 1.2 the particular construals are marked generally as ct_x (construal from text part x). That way, we can appreciate another general property of DST: the tight interface of the "construed" and the "real." The construed indirect meanings do not arise independently but from the interplay of literal meanings of events in the text which are performed by physical entities in real time. These include entities and events such as "our allies," "Sarajevo," "end of Cold War," and "the Second World War," which are assigned to the spatial and temporal axes. In other words, the DST model captures, side by side, inferences from dated, individual events, as well as more sophisticated inferences from different configurations of these events interpreted as meaningful by the addressee. For example, the positioning on the spatial and temporal axes of such entities and events as "Sarajevo," "Kosovo," "the First World War," "the Second World War," and "end of Cold War" allows representation of a forceful analogy salient in the text. On the *t* axis, the geopolitical and historical space is extended "backwards," metonymically, by reference to the location "Sarajevo." Kosovo is linked to Sarajevo, and Sarajevo is linked metonymically to the First World War, and the First World War to the Second World War and the Holocaust. These links can be considered metonymic since the relation between Kosovo, Sarajevo, and the First World War is one of conceptual "contiguity" in a geopolitical frame that holds events progressing from the remote past toward the present. The mention of "Sarajevo" is used to evoke the whole First World War frame, and "this region" is used in the same metonymic way to evoke Second World War and the Holocaust frames. The consecutive construals are marked in Figure 1.2 by the five ct_x spaces (including sentence numbers in the original version) connected by the *metonymy* link. The right-most space represents the final and most important construal forced by the text. On this construal, the developments in Kosovo may constitute a global threat, and the threat may be just as big as the analogies with the past have shown.

Producing analyses such as the aforementioned ones, the DST model offers excellent insights in the representation and positioning of entities in political discourse. First, it recognizes the fundamental role of distance from the US entities in conceptualizing other entities and events in discourse generally. Obvious as this may seem, it is a vital prerequisite for any further inquiry in the ways of construing distant objects and happenings as close to the speaker and her audience. Consequently, it is a prerequisite for studying patterns of coercion that build upon the contraction of the *Us*-vs.-*Them* (or *Them*-vs.-*Us*) distance. Second, it acknowledges that the distance is relative and that it is symbolically represented through discourse. This makes possible further explorations in how the coercive mental representations can be evoked through linguistic means for pragmatic effects. Third, the DST model shows that "distance" involves a number of mutually interactive dimensions, and thus the representations of entities and events arise from a combined activation of different cognitive domains such as spatial, temporal and modal.

There are at the same time some unattended issues, which have been inspiring further research. DST can be described as a model of the default organization of entities in sociopolitical discourse space. The aim of DST is, by Chilton's (2004) own admission, to show how people's mental representations are positioned relative to the three cognitive dimensions s, t, m. It is not to show how people *are made* to establish representations that match the pragmatic goals of the speaker. The DST model does not account for categories of lexico-grammatical items responsible for positioning entities and events at different and thus measurable distances from the deictic center. As a result, it does not account for the intensity of pragmatic powers, including the power to deliver a threat, exerted by these entities and events on the US camp. On the one hand, DST recognizes the ideological, legitimizing, coercive, etc. discourse roles of certain words and expressions. On the other, it arbitrarily assigns them a static position on one of the three axes, in a set distance from the deictic center. In consequence, conceptual shifts from the periphery of the discourse space to the center are not accounted for. There is little way within DST to determine which linguistic items, in what numbers, and within which dimension, are the most effective in forcing a given representation (such as a coercive threatening arrangement) on the addressee. These missing issues of lexicalization and linguistic grounding are taken very seriously in the later models.

1.4.2. Political Metaphor

The term "political metaphor" (PM) refers in the present book to a set of approaches and strands of thought in CDS that build upon insights from conceptual metaphor theory (CMT) (Lakoff and Johnson 1980; Johnson 1987; etc.) to develop critical agendas and new tools for the study of metaphor-based discourse within the political arena (e.g., Charteris-Black 2005; Musolff and Zinken 2009). In particular, it refers to approaches such as Musolff's (2016) and Koller's (2014), involving the analysis, in political and discursive terms, of *conceptual scenarios*. The scenarios are understood as largely conventionalized and in many ways automatic patterns of understanding based on embodied experience. As such, they endorse seemingly self-evident default conclusions and further some "natural" and "obvious" behaviors, actions, or solutions. Compared with other domains of metaphor use and analysis, in political discourse conceptual master scenarios (such as PROBLEM IS ENEMY or POLITICAL CONFLICT IS WAR) often reveal a pragmatic "added value." Not only do they denote and explain their target concepts but they can also express evaluation of a topic or reassure the addressee that a perceived threat or problem fits into a familiar experience pattern and thus can be dealt with by familiar problem-solving strategies.

In his comprehensive account of political metaphor, Musolff (2016) describes how the NATION/STATE IS CONTAINER scenario has been used (and abused) in the UK to force simplistic patterns of reasoning with regard to immigration issues.[2] He summarizes the scenario as follows:

> The state [UK] is conceptualized as a *container* with distinct *boundaries*, which separate those *on the outside* from those *inside*; immigrants are thus *outsiders* who want to *come/move into the container*. The *container* is often conceptualized as a *building* that has *doors* and other openings that can be *closed, open* or *half-open*; it is also seen as a vessel that has a *limited capacity* to include contents; if too many immigrants come in, this increases the *pressure* inside to *bursting point* and necessitates the erection of new *barriers*. (Musolff 2016: 82–3)

The argument in the scenario presents the immigration issue and the "solution" in familiar, black-and-white terms. The threat to the state-container is well defined and the course of action to prevent the threat is equally well defined: apparently, it is enough to "close the doors" to stop the problem. Both the premise and the conclusion in the argument are grounded in the embodied experience that people have with bounded spaces. This experience makes acceptance of the solution pattern quite automatic. Other notable cases of argumentation based on political metaphor show that such automaticity often relies further on the portrayal of the "outsider-invader" in essentially negative terms. The most extreme and infamous example is the discourse of far-right nationalists in post–First World War Germany, who identified Jews as social parasites on the German and other European nations, which needed to be eliminated. This racist conceptualization involved not only the STATE IS CONTAINER scenario but, principally, its combination with another master scenario, in which STATE is perceived in terms of BODY. The STATE IS BODY scenario was included mainly for the purposes of moral justification and policy legitimization. One of the main messages of the metaphor was that, just as illnesses or infections to the body meet with a quick and well-defined response, so should the "illnesses" or "infections" to the state.

The focus on scenario analysis makes political metaphor an excellent research handle on the discourse of conflict and crisis and threat-based rhetoric, which can be applied independently or, crucially, in combination with other analytical models. Involving a systematic study of lexical choices enacting the particular master scenarios (such as the items and phrases developing the CONTAINER scenario), PM provides a considerable compensation for the deficit in lexical grounding of models such as discourse space theory. Notably, PM has its lens on the linguistic marking of entities that constitute the in- and out-group (*Us* and *Them*) camps and thus warrants a rich account of cases where metaphor partakes in the coding of social or geopolitical differences and the resulting distance. In consequence, PM sheds light on the extreme cases in which the aforementioned differences lead to conflict and clash. Since the way in which the opposing camps are defined (e.g., as less or more antagonistic to each other) decides about the dynamics of the conflict, political metaphor is also a tool to elucidate, in linguistic terms, the caliber of the threat involved.

There are also analytical benefits that go beyond the account of discourse space relations. Discussing issues of political propaganda, we noted the importance of intertextuality and "shareability" of content in maximizing the uptake of speaker's message. Metaphor-based communication can be described as inherently shareable, as metaphoric discourses provide insights that are rhetorically attractive, make an emotional appeal, and are thus easily remembered and recirculated. The uptake is even easier when metaphors get integrated as scenario narratives (as they mostly do), complete with apparently obvious conclusions motivating specific actions. Approaches such as Musolff's (2016) offer a comprehensive view and explanation of the propagandistic and coercive powers of metaphor. They show that, in many situations, a metaphor does not just create reality but becomes "a guide for future action" (Lakoff and Johnson 1980, in Musolff 2016: 2). Such actions naturally fit the metaphor, which in turn reinforces the power of the metaphor to make experience coherent. In this sense, as observed by PM models, metaphors can be self-fulfilling prophecies, ensuring long life of a given propaganda text or discourse.

Finally, PM approaches point to the usual consistency of metaphor-based discourse with the audience predispositions. We have seen that a core element of political communication that aims at successful policy legitimization and popular support is the anchoring of the communication in the sociopolitical, ideological, or moral ground presented as common to the audience and the speaker/leader. Since the source of all metaphors is cognitive experience, metaphor-based discourse demonstrates an intrinsic attachment to sociocognitive relations and arrangements that have evolved naturally in society and thus remain uncontested. A good example is the concept of FAMILY (Musolff 2016: 25ff), underlying such metaphoric scenarios as NATION IS FAMILY or STATE IS FAMILY. As the use of FAMILY attributes to depict STATE features and relations is hardly questioned, the metaphor constitutes a powerful tool to enact unity and inner solidarity of the *Us* camp, particularly useful in mobilizing the *Us* entities to stand up to an external threat.

1.4.3. Proximization Theory

Similar to the DST and PM models, *proximization* recognizes the existence of the discourse space (DS) and the principal distinction between the *Us* and *Them* camps positioned in the mutually opposite (central vs. remote) locations of the DS. As a strategy, proximization consists in presenting the "remote *Them*" (distant entities, events, states of affairs, and "distant," i.e., adversarial ideologies) as increasingly closer and eventually threatening to the "central *Us*" (the speaker and her audience). It thus involves a forced construal of *movement* of the antagonistic *Them* entities in the direction of the *Us* entities. As a forced construal operation, proximization demonstrates substantial coercive powers, which can be applied in the service of sociopolitical goals. Crucially, by projecting the *Them* entities as encroaching upon the *Us* camp (both physical and ideological), the speaker aims to legitimize consequential actions that she declares to be the best preventive measures to stop the invasion (Figure 1.3).

The term "proximization" was originally proposed to analyze coercion patterns in the US anti-terrorist rhetoric following 9/11 (Cap 2006, 2008, 2010). Since then it has been used within different discourse domains, though most commonly in studies of state-political discourses: crisis construction and war rhetoric (Chovanec 2010), anti-migration discourse (Hart 2010), political party representation (Cienki, Kaal and Maks 2010), construction of national memory (Filardo Llamas 2010), and design of foreign policy documents (Dunmire 2011). In his proposal for proximization

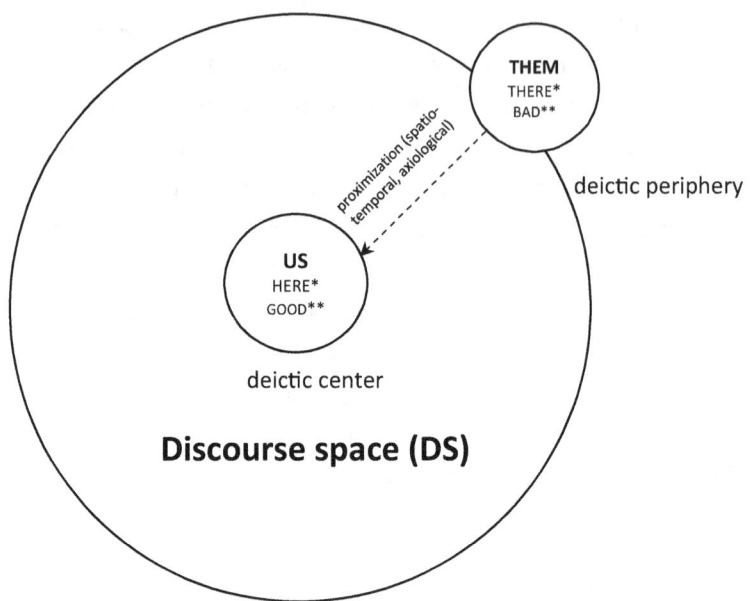

* center-periphery opposites in spatial and temporal proximization
**center-periphery opposites in axiological proximization

Figure 1.3 Proximization in discourse space.

theory (PT), Cap (2013, 2017) argues for three complementary aspects of proximization: spatial, temporal, and axiological. According to Cap (2013), "spatial proximization" is a forced construal of *Them* entities encroaching physically on the *Us* entities in deictic center of the DS. Analogically to Chilton's DST, the spatial aspect of proximization is considered primary as the remaining aspects involve conceptualizations in spatial terms. "Temporal proximization" is a construal of the *Them*-vs.-*Us* conflict as not only imminent, but also momentous, historic, and thus requiring immediate response and unique preventive measures. Spatial and temporal proximizations involve fear appeals (becoming particularly strong in reactionary political projects) and typically use analogies to conflate the growing threat with an actual disastrous occurrence in the past endorsing the current scenario. "Axiological proximization" is a construal of growing conflict between values, ideals, and ideological postures of members of the *Us* and *Them* camps. While the conflict is construed as initially ideological, its long-term effects involve a threat of materialization of the hostile values in the *Us* camp.

Although all uses of proximization in discourse involve presence of linguistic choices performing all the three strategies, spatial, temporal, and axiological, the degree to which each strategy is represented depends on its pragmatic strength and effectiveness in the current context. This means that contextual changes, such as new events or geopolitical developments, may cause the speaker to limit the use of one strategy and to compensate it by an increased use of another, in the interest of the continuity of legitimization. Such regularities have been documented in studies on the evolution of anti-terrorist discourse after 9/11 (Dunmire 2011; Cap 2017; Oddo 2018). As observed in Cap (2017), in geopolitical context of high public anxiety and fear (for instance in the aftermath of a terrorist attack), the strategy of spatial proximization is preferred to a more "moderate" axiological proximization. Conversely, the latter strategy takes over when anxiety levels decrease and there is no longer a specific entity, event, or a flashback vision that could be used as the premise for threat construction and fear appeal.

It is, however, possible to find examples where different proximization strategies are used sequentially within a brief stretch of discourse. This happens in discourses that start by making a call for action on *ideological* reasons and then alert the audience to harsh *material* consequences of ignoring these reasons. In such discourses the first part involves, normally, axiological proximization, and the second spatiotemporal proximization. As discussed in Koller et al. (2019) and Cap (2019), this pattern was extensively used by Nigel Farage, the leader of the United Kingdom Independence Party, in the weeks before and after the Brexit referendum in June 2016. In an interview at BBC on July 16, Farage calls for strong anti-migration measures in the interest of Britain's security, which, as he argues, has been put at risk during the UK's recent years of membership in the EU:

> We refuse to sacrifice our freedom and security for political correctness. We must call things by their true names. Rather than shedding tears like Federica Mogherini or organizing marches that solve nothing, the state should ensure the safety of its citizens. (. . .) To those who are happy to welcome immigrants at our doors, I have a suggestion: go and see the refugee camps in Turkey. See the gangs and the riots. See the young Muslim criminals. See the anger, violence, and terror. It is there and is ready for export. This kind of evil might not have reached us yet, but it is well in sight. And there is no-one in Brussels who can protect us when it comes. (Nigel Farage at BBC station, July 17, 2016)

Farage's text identifies *Them* as non-EU migrants and in particular Muslim immigrant groups from the Middle East and North Africa. This identification allows a legitimate use of radical rhetoric, which draws upon the aura of fear instilled by the recent terrorist attacks and other criminal acts involving Islamic perpetrators. Specifically, Farage refers to the July 2016 attack in Nice, criticizing EU's passivity and the lack of proper response ("Rather than shedding tears like Federica Mogherini [EU Foreign Minister] or organizing marches that solve nothing, the state should ensure the safety of its citizens").[3] The strongest fear appeal comes in a narrative that develops in the second part of the text (from "To those who are happy. . ." until the end of the text). This narrative includes two consecutive segments, "ideological" and "material," which progress in a linear fashion to form a causative structure. The first segment ("refugee camps in Turkey (. . .) gangs and the riots (. . .) young Muslim criminals (. . .) anger, violence, and terror. It is there and is ready for export") provides social context and conditions for the emergence of threat coming from the *Them* camp. The second segment ("This kind of evil might not have reached us yet, but it is well in sight") changes the ontology of that threat, from being a "remote possibility" to making "actual presence" in the *Us* camp ("is well in sight"). As we have noted, such a dynamic construal involves both axiological and spatiotemporal proximizations, or, in fact, a sequentially structured interplay of the two. While the initial axiological proximization forces the conceptualization of a relatively distant vision based upon a specific contextual arrangement, the subsequent spatiotemporal proximization turns that threatening vision into a material threat, resulting in a virtually inevitable invasion ("when it comes"). To perform this conceptual shift by lexical and grammatical means, a modality change is used in the text—a "possibility-setting" *might*-phrase ("might not have reached us yet") leads to a "realistic" *be*-phrase ("is well in sight").

The study of Farage's interview[4] is a fine sample of the methodological potential of proximization to produce, together with the other approaches, some truly multidimensional critical research in conflict discourse. Analogically to the DST and PM models, proximization takes the ideological and persuasive potential of discourse not as a property of language itself but of the underlying cognitive processes that language reflects and mobilizes. As a development on these models, it subsumes a dynamic view of discourse space that involves not only the opposition between the *Us* and *Them* camps, but also the discursively constructed movement of the *Them* entities toward the *Us* entities. Furthermore, it provides a linguistic focus on the lexical choices that political speakers (leaders) make in order to index the existing ideological distinctions and, crucially, to demonstrate the capacity of the *Them* entities to erase these distinctions by forcibly colonizing the US camp. In that sense, proximization is a complex model of coercion, threat construction, and legitimization of political leadership.

Altogether, the research program promoted by the DST, PM, and PT models sets them apart from the many other theories arising from the CDS family (Zienkowski et al. 2011; Angermuller et al. 2014). Most importantly, it challenges the traditional (Buehler 1934; Bar-Hillel 1954) view of deixis, on which deictic markers are considered merely a technical necessity for the possible interpretability of a language, rather than a true instrument of strategic communication that involves persuasion, legitimization, and social coercion. Contesting the conception of deixis as a finite repository of "deictic expressions," the DST, PM, and PT models take a much broader approach to deictic markers. On this new approach, deictic markers can be treated as not just formal tools for the coding of static elements of context, but as essential elements of deictic shifts and forced construals of distance. Naturally, the DST, PM, and PT models reveal differences with regard to how strongly this position is articulated and how extensively it is described. Here, Chilton's DST can be considered a precursor, defining the main role of deixis in providing symbolic representations of relative distance in discourse. This account is elaborated on in the PM and PT models, which go on to describe deictic shifts in terms of set lexical items and phrases that can be extracted from a text corpus. Altogether, we can say that the explanatory powers of the three approaches are complementary, responding to the main challenges of political communication, particularly those posed by conflict and crisis discourses. The studies in the empirical parts of the book (Chapters 3–6) are thus essentially eclectic, involving tools and insights from all the three models.

2

Polish Contexts

Threat-Based Communication and Crisis Management in Communist and Post-Communist Poland

In the opening chapter we identified several mechanisms and concepts involved in the enactment of political leadership, such as coercion, legitimization, delegitimization, propaganda, and credibility. We have observed that political visions and policies are often presented to the public in terms of responses to urgent matters of attention that people find personally consequential and potentially threatening. This establishes conflict and threat generation, as well as management of the resulting crisis, as central instruments of policy legitimization. We have discussed relevant research models, such as discourse space theory, political metaphor, and proximization, offering workable tools to analyze various forms and manifestations of these ploys in discourse. Such an analysis will take place in Chapters 3–6, where we focus on the discourse of the right-wing political leadership in contemporary Poland, in relation to other modern European discourses. The present chapter is an introduction to this study, providing a historical perspective on the evolution of fear-based communication in Poland after the Second World War. It shows that, despite some predictable differences related to changing historical context, Polish postwar leaders (as well as the state-controlled media) have been consistent in claiming legitimization of policies based on discursively motivated social mobilization against a developing threat. The result is a firm entrenchment in the Polish public space of the *Them*-vs.-*Us* conflict categories, and the tendency of consecutive leaders to fill in these categories according to current political interests and affiliations. Though such a tendency is not alien to other European countries, and the countries of Central Europe in particular, the special thing about Poland is that not only do its leaders take rhetorical advantage of the aura of crisis but they themselves provoke conflictual and crisis situations, home and abroad, to propose "solutions" and thus legitimate their leadership.

2.1. The Communist Years (1945–89): Postwar Threats, Public Fears, and Social Mobilization

While the Second World War, still in the living memory of many Poles, can be considered the most traumatic period in Poland's history and thus an inexhaustible source of public discourse, the centuries before the war were just as turbulent. Placed geographically between the West and the East, between two giants, Germany and Russia, Poland has always had to prove its right to exist. Yet, a small kingdom at the cross-roads, Poland developed into a superpower in the sixteenth century, with its borders extending to the Black Sea and its sights trained on the throne in Moscow. Some 200 years later, however, Poland, a victim of its "gentry democracy" paralyzing the state institutions by indecisiveness (Galasińska and Galasiński 2010), vanished from the map. Russia, Prussia, and Austria in successive decades of the latter part of the eighteenth century annexed more and more of Polish territory, until it disappeared—for the next 120 years. These 120 years of lost independence mark one of the mythologically crucial periods in Polish history. Having brought endless uprisings and independence battles, they are regarded as the best period of Polish literature, one which likens Poland to the Messiah of nations and views the country's suffering as redeeming of the world's ills. This romantic tradition is still very much vivid in Polish mythology, inspiring various public and private discourses (Jaworski and Galasiński 1998).

The end of the First World War in 1918 brought a new beginning for Polish statehood. The success was commonly attributed to Marshal Józef Piłsudski—a leader who is still the paragon to be emulated by today's politicians (most notably Jarosław Kaczyński, the leader of the Law & Justice party). Life in the new Poland was far from idyllic, however. Soviet Russia's attack in 1920 resulted in the "miracle on the Vistula river," a battle termed by Edgar Vincent as the eighteenth decisive battle of the world (Galasińska and Galasiński 2010). The

Polish army led by Piłsudski defeated the Russian army marching westward. Also the internal political scene was far from ideal, plunging in chaos after assassination of the first Polish president Gabriel Narutowicz. In response, Piłsudski took a firm grip over the country with his coup d'état in 1926. What followed was an authoritarian rule never far away from the army, increasingly anti-communist and often plainly aggressive (peaking with the annexation of a part of Czechoslovakia in 1938). The outbreak of the Second World War put an end to that period, beginning the national nightmare of more than five years, in which time 6 million Poles lost their lives and most of the country, its resources and infrastructure, got completely destroyed.

The significance of the Second World War in contemporary Poland is huge, and war-related themes continue to pervade different domains of Polish public discourse, occasionally extending beyond Polish borders as well. For example, in 2007 Jarosław Kaczyński (then a prime minister), when negotiating new voting arrangements in the European Union stated that Poland should be assessed in terms of the population it might have had, had it not been for the war. Even though condemned by many, Kaczyński "struck a very raw chord" (Galasińska and Galasiński 2010: 7). There are still many Poles who are hurt, who feel wronged, for whom the war is still very much a living and extremely relevant context. Thus the meta-narratives of the Second World War abound in stories of Polish bravery, with the battles of Monte Cassino or the Warsaw Uprising as the pinnacles of Polish heroism.

That said, it is easy to appreciate the leading role of the Second World War in Polish public discourse immediately after the war—that is, after the German surrender and the formation, under Soviet control, of the first postwar government in 1945. For that first government, almost completely dependent on orders from the Kremlin, the devastation brought by the war was so much an economic and sociopolitical challenge, as an instrument of social mobilization and coercion. First of all, it sanctioned the state propaganda drawing on the dominant postwar fears, such as hunger, crime, extreme poverty, and unemployment. Yet even more crucially, it allowed the government to induce and stimulate other, virtual fears, such as news about a pending new world war and Polish homes endangered by external enemies (Kamiński 2016). Such threatening discourses would fall, then, on highly fertile ground, not only in Poland. The all-European scale of the phenomenon was thoroughly examined by Keith Lowe (2012). Analyzing the traumatic legacy of war, the postwar need for vengeance, the plague of ethnic cleansings and civil wars, which broke out across Europe in the late 1940s and the 1950s, Lowe (2012) concludes that all those horrible experiences derived from the postwar "savagery" of Europeans. The postwar Europe, argues Lowe, was a continent inhabited by demoralized people who in the course of the war became used to maneuvering in the labyrinth constituted by famine, massive destruction, and omnipresent violence. In consequence, deprived of state institutions, they tried to soften their own concerns and isolation by supporting totalitarian governments or even joining their structures and organizations (Arendt 1958; Lefebvre 1974).

In Poland, communist propaganda maintained that the best antidote to the postwar condition, with all its fears and anxiety, was just loyal attachment to the communist rule. Attempting to teach Poles the "proper socialist emotional model" (Kersten 1984), it associated the sense of national safety and the social and personal well-being with communist ideology and the Polish-Soviet friendship. At the same time, it produced messages abounding in different types of threats that were supposed to be instructive about proper and improper "socialist behavior." Kamiński (2016) argues that the majority of threat-based messages traveled along four interconnected communication channels involving four thematic domains. These main domains were: (i) the continuing German threat, (ii) foreign (mostly American) conspiracy and espionage, (iii) American economic war and cultural threat, and (iv) the third world war and nuclear threat. All of them were in fact modeled on the concurrent Soviet discourse, making ample references to the Second World War (Kersten 1984).

2.1.1. The German Threat

The capitulation of Nazi Germany changed hardly anything with regard to the sense of fear associated with the former oppressor. After the war, Polish communist government and the state press made the occupied zones of Germany the main focus of attention, reporting on the rebuilding projects, especially those under the American administration, in terms of "dangerous resurrection of German militarism" (Express Ilustrowany, December 11, 1946). Such visions gradually assumed a strategic propagandistic purpose. They served to evoke public anxiety and fear, inspiring reliance on the new government to protect national security and individual safety of the people

(Kamiński 2016). The motif of the ongoing remilitarization of Germany was perpetuated in the press by hard-hitting headers, such as "German army practices in English occupation zone," announcing the ominous news of "more than 120 thousand German soldiers and officers having the Prussian spirit of imperialism and militarism standing ready for action" (Express Ilustrowany, December 30, 1946). Similar warnings were heard in speeches by the top politicians. Soon after becoming the prime minister, Józef Cyrankiewicz said in a famous radio address that "the Western administrators are in fact supporting the rebuilding of the German military and German economy instead of punishing Nazi criminals" (February 20, 1947). Finally, fears of German revival resonated in numerous satirical drawings published in papers such as *Express Ilustrowany* and *Głos Robotniczy*, especially after the Byrnes-Bevin agreement.[1] For instance, the drawing titled "In the British Occupation Zone" showed Nazi troops, fully mobilized and visibly ready to fight, marching in front of British officers (Express Ilustrowany, January 20, 1947).

The establishment of two German states in 1949 made these fear appeals even stronger, placing them fully in line with other coercive strategies of the state propaganda. The communist press regularly reported on former officers of the SS and the Gestapo as well as war criminals who were involved with Western occupants in rebuilding the German administration and army (Kamiński 2016). The aura of fear grew substantially after the United States officially announced the idea of the rearmament of West Germany. Implemented in January 1950, the plan was supposed to balance the growing Soviet military power in Europe. The response of the Polish government was immediate and loud. In his ninety-minute address to the Central Committee of the Polish United Workers' Party in late January, President Bolesław Bierut made it clear: "We will not allow the rebuilding of the Wehrmacht, we will not allow remilitarizing the murderers of our mothers, wives and children, we will not accept the rearmament of the hangmen of our nation, destroyers of our capital city, towns and villages" (January 28, 1950). It is considered that Bierut's speech initiated significant radicalization of the state propaganda, defining its domains, targets, and the main channels for the next few years (Prażmowska 2010). The overarching strategy was to conflate West Germany, the United States, as well as the majority of Western European countries (especially Britain and France) into one common "enemy camp," posing a direct threat to the "Socialist family of nations," as Bierut put it in his party speech. This new strategy was duly adopted by the press, which produced multiple frightening examples of "anti-Socialist collaboration" between the enemy countries. The collaboration between West Germany and the United States was, of course, the most salient motif, involving countless stories of American engagement (mostly financial) in the rebuilding of German military power. In newspapers, satirical drawings were published showing the United States spend their money to, literally, "plant" military infrastructure in West Germany. Such images proved extremely effective, inducing public fears and facilitating the acceptance of policies proposed by the government as preemptive measures to neutralize the gathering threat. Typically, they involved visual proximization (Kopytowska et al. 2017), making the threat particularly tangible and appealing. As a result, they paved the way for multimodal coercion strategies employing a mix of visual and textual techniques that we can still frequently spot in the contemporary political discourse in Poland. We return to this interesting issue in later chapters.

2.1.2. American "Conspiracy" and "Espionage"

As has been noted, the communist propaganda of the early 1950s followed a relatively consolidated vision of the adversary, seeing the "Western world" and "capitalist imperialism" generally as the source of all threat. Gradually, however, the main villain role came to be ascribed to America, partly because of important international developments (such as the US intervention in Korea), partly due to internal economic situation, and partly to "compensate" for the somewhat diminishing appeal of the German threat in the second half of the decade. As memories of the war were becoming more and more remote, there emerged a need to redefine and concretize the enemy to keep social mobilization, stamina, and loyalty to the state at a continual high (Prażmowska 2010). The unconditional approval of state policies was in fact the necessary condition for successful realization of a number of massive economic projects, such as the construction of steelworks in Kraków's district of Nowa Huta, the development of shipyards in Gdańsk and Szczecin, and the opening of the Passenger Automobile Factory in Warsaw. Still, despite the officially announced success of these and other ventures, and in spite of the growth of economic indexes emphasized in the press, everyday life of Polish people in the 1950s was extremely tough. For example, the average salary in 1955 was nearly 20% lower than in 1938, and the number of flats available in many of the bombed cities matched only 30% of the demand of the growing Polish postwar population (Zaremba 2006). The most important concern disturbing Poles in the 1950s was, however, the lack of basic goods on the market: the empty shelves in shops selling such basic articles as food, clothes, or even soap became the symbol of inefficiency of the socialist economy. These concerns only deepened with the increase in the prices of meat, coal, and other vital products ordered by the government in 1954.

Consequently, in an attempt to turn people's attention away from these difficulties, the communist government resorted to vivid propaganda figures representing external, mostly American, threats of conspiracy and espionage. Instilling the aura of American spy-mania was a vital part of the strategy to explain the problems that the government was unable to solve. Thus, the figures of spies were often presented as agents of economic deterioration responsible for the sabotage suppressing the economic development of Poland. Furthermore, the motif of spy-mania fomented by propaganda served as a convenient pretext justifying the communist terror and brutal political and military fights against all adversaries of the new regime regularly accused of running conspiratorial activity. As a result of these accusations, in 1954, thirty-three persons were found guilty of espionage and eleven were sentenced to death in Warsaw alone. According to Kamiński (2016), the years 1954–5 saw the very peak of the spy-mania, manifested in the unprecedented number of propaganda messages, including governmental addresses to the nation, radio broadcasts, anti-American speeches at public events and ceremonies (such as the grand opening of the tenth Anniversary Stadium in Warsaw), countless press articles, and, not least, street posters. For the best appeal, the latter were often placed next to offices and factories, or along busy pedestrianized streets. In a famous poster image (see Kamiński 2016), the "spy" is symbolized by ominous shadow of a person waiting for an occasion to attack the Polish worker. A text above the spy figure says, "Guard your professional secrecies!," continuing, "YOU might be the enemy target" at the bottom.

2.1.3. American Economic War and Cultural Threat

The threat of American conspiracy and espionage was perpetuated alongside with other more or less virtual threats, such as the vision of gathering economic conflict, ideological encroachment, and cultural dominance. Following the rejection of the Marshall Plan in March 1948, Soviet leaders issued precise instructions for countries of the Socialist bloc on how to respond to offers of American economic help and cooperation, including offers of humanitarian aid provided under the supervision of international bodies such as UNNRA.[2] Polish communist government showed their loyalty by rejecting most of such aid "in order to protect the country from the capitalist hegemony of the American economy," as PM Józef Cyrankiewicz boldly declared in a radio address (Cyrankiewicz, January 6, 1949). Moreover, after implementation of the Marshall Plan in Italy, France, Spain, and West Germany, communist propaganda started to present the plan as an American attempt to subordinate Western economies to the finance of Wall Street. Numerous press articles and propaganda movies presented an image of Europe divided into imperialist and anti-democratic Western Europe, which embraced the plan, and anti-imperialist and democratic socialist nations which rejected the plan. The Marshall Plan was also pictured as a synonym of American capitalism, a symbol of inequality, of oppression of the working class, and the antithesis of progressive socialism. Thus, from a discourse analytical perspective, the anti-plan rhetoric in postwar Poland made a major contribution to strengthening the geopolitical mindset based on the "*Us* and *Them*" polarization.

It should be noted at this point that instilling anti-American attitudes in Polish people was never an easy task. In his comprehensive study of communist propaganda between 1945 and 1970, Zaremba (2006) quotes Aleksander Kowalski, the first secretary of the Polish United Workers' Party in Warsaw, who said the following at a party meeting in 1952:

> Among Polish youth there is a lot of sentiment towards the United States. It results from the fact that Poland never had any conflict with the USA. The fact that our peasants migrated to the USA, that many Poles receive dollars in letters from their families in America creates the image of the USA as a state of wealthy people who even after World War Two are rich enough to send flour to their families in Poland. In Poland we have Hoover's Squares, American movies, literature. All of this is living in consciousness of our youth and generates strong sentiment towards the USA. It also generates a lack of understanding of the fact that the USA is becoming an enemy of our nation, an enemy of our sovereignty. (Zaremba 2006: 45)

Such concerns, however, only strengthened the determination of the communist government:

> New Poland was created in the fight for independence against Hitlerism, but from the very first moment of our independence we are struggling to establish and solidify democracy against American imperialism. We must make our society aware of this fact, at all costs. (PM Cyrankiewicz in Express Ilustrowany, November 18, 1954)

During the 1950s the communist media went out of their way to realize this mission. Anti-American propaganda reached its peak in the middle of the decade, announcing, in a near-hysterical tone, the approach of American "economic war" on Poland. The "proof" was the invasion, in summer 1954, of a potato bug named (nomen omen) "Colorado beetle" on Polish potato fields, for which Washington was allegedly responsible. The Party newspaper *Trybuna Ludu* deemed the invasion "an incredible crime of American imperialists," arguing that the fast-spreading pest was a "subversive-conspiratorial activity inflicted against socialist Poland through mass consumption of potato crops" (Trybuna Ludu, August 14, 1954). Drawing on the fear of hunger still present in Polish society in the 1950s, the propaganda campaign stressing American responsibility for the mass invasion of the beetle turned out extremely successful. Notably, the threat posed by the beetle was often presented as a developing worldwide problem (Kamiński 2016). For example, in September 1954 the newspaper *Szpilki* published a satirical drawing of the beetle seen as a mutation of the "Uncle Sam" figure. The creature, wearing a typical top hat with an American flag pattern, was pictured as an aggressive predator equipped with sharp teeth and tentacles giving the monster a literally global range (Szpilki, September 16, 1954).

The image of American interference in the Polish postwar economy was often constructed in relation to a broader image of American sociocultural invasion on Polish values, national legacy, and everyday life of the people. The concept of a transatlantic sociocultural threat proved in fact quite resistant to geopolitical changes, fueling anti-American (and anti-Western in general) propaganda until the end of the communist rule in 1989. If there is one example that perfectly sums up the many ways in which the threat was communicated over these years, it is the expressive caricature of "American newspaper" produced by Bronisław Linke, a Warsaw satirist known for his zealous support for the communist rule. In 1961, Linke made a drawing of a fictional American daily announcing the news saturated with almost all types of violence—from racist crimes to regular brutal banditry. The relaxed posture of the reader (also included in the drawing) was supposed to suggest that Americans became used to being exposed to such horrific news on a daily basis. Among the scenes pictured by Linke, the view of a Black male hanging on a rope "attached" to the slogan "America for whites" was probably the most shocking. It suggested that aggression, violence, and intolerance were deeply ingrained in the mentality of the vast majority of Americans, leading to the formation of a dangerous warlike society posing a direct threat to global peace.

2.1.4. The Threat of the Third World War

Among the many different, less, and more virtual fears stimulated in the Polish society by consecutive communist governments, the fear of a gathering nuclear crisis and the third world war was apparently the most permanent. It derived, also, from the most realistic premises and geopolitical factors, such as international conflicts, wars, and the threatening arms race throughout the Cold War. According to Prażmowska (2010), the fear of a pending third world war was particularly strong during four periods: the war in Korea (1950–3), the Cuban missile crisis in 1962, the US massacre at Mai Lai during the Vietnam War in 1968,[3] and the early years (1985–6) of implementation of the so-called Reagan Doctrine aimed at "rolling back" the pro-communist governments in Africa, Asia, and Latin America. In all these periods, propaganda activity was at a continual high, inducing and perpetuating the fear in the service of social mobilization for different goals defined by the government. One goal was to instill public anger toward the American "war provokers" (PM Cyrankiewicz in Trybuna Ludu, February 6, 1968) and thus foster support to the communist government as a guarantor of safety. Using vivid slogans, such as "The entire progressive humanity protests against the imperialist aggression in Vietnam" (Trybuna Ludu, February 21, 1968), communists agitators encouraged workers to express their anger in the form of mass protests organized throughout Poland. Such calls from the government and the communist press were often successful; in the first weeks of the Vietnam War, 100,000 people demonstrated in Warsaw against the "imperialist aggression," reacting with enthusiasm when news of resistance of the Vietcong forces were announced (Kamiński 2016). Although the Warsaw crowd did not gather spontaneously, the propagandists still managed to communicate directly to the workers the official interpretation of the war (Kemp-Welch 2008).

The other goal was more practical, involving transformation of the fear and anger into an increased fervor to work. The communist media claimed that the workplace should be seen as a battlefield where each worker, using his regular tools, could efficiently fight against the war provokers. Originally coined during the Korean War, the battlefield metaphor survived in the communist discourse until the mid-1980s. Over that period, it was salient in pompous slogans such as "We, the working people of Kraków and Nowa Huta, are all soldiers on the great front of confrontation with the Western enemies of socialism" (Trybuna Ludu, March 6, 1969) or "With the increased efficiency of work, Polish working class responds to the US-instigated revolt in Nicaragua" (Trybuna Ludu, June 2, 1985). These bombastic declarations and calls appeared not only in the press, but also in numerous pro-peace resolutions announced by workers in thousands of workplaces across Poland.

Judging from the massive number of such resolutions, the phantom of a next global (and very likely nuclear) conflict was, most of the time, extremely realistic. Over years, it provided communist leaders of Poland with some unique opportunities for policy legitimization and effective management of all kinds of economic as well as political crises. Interestingly, propaganda producers were often able to manufacture the atomic threat—through metaphor and other means—in the interest of apparently unrelated ventures. For example, for a long time one of the most popular slogans used by communist agitators was a simple rhyme—"W odpowiedzi na atomy budujemy nowe domy!" ["In response to atomic bombs we are building new houses"]—chanted at the numerous mass meetings in Polish factories and offices. The aura of fear of a possible external invasion was equally helpful in inspiring the spirit of resistance, increasing national pride, and even boosting performance of Polish athletes at international competitions. One would think all this must have changed completely with the end of the communist rule in 1989. Not quite—by the time most of the old threats had disappeared, new fears and anxieties emerged, quickly entering the public discourse.

2.2. Social Conflict and Threat-Based Communication in the Third Republic

The year 1989 saw re-establishment of pluralist parliamentary democracy, marking the beginning of the "Third Republic," the period named so to emphasize its connection to the two previous periods of Poland's freedom and independence (before the eighteenth-century partitions and between the two world wars). This momentous change happened after the so-called Round Table talks between representatives of the outgoing communist government and the Polish United Workers' Party, and "Solidarity"—originally a trade union but effectively a massive social movement including dissident intellectuals and supported by the Roman Catholic Church. The first (partially) free elections took place in June 1989, giving rise to the first non-communist government in the Eastern bloc, with Tadeusz Mazowiecki (representing the Solidarity side during the Round Table negotiations) as the prime minister. One year later, the leader of Solidarity in the 1980s and the Nobel Peace Prize winner of 1983 Lech Wałęsa became the president of Poland, thus locking the unprecedented change that inspired democratic transitions in countries of the entire post-Soviet camp (Raś 2017).

The beginning of a new democratic era did not mean, however, the end of sociopolitical divisions and the related anxieties. Important as it was, the Round Table compromise set up a strong divide between "post-communist" and "post-Solidarity" political forces for years to come. The first symbol of this divide was the composition of Mazowiecki's cabinet. Months after the June 1989 elections, representatives of the previous regime still controlled some of the most important offices. For example, the ministries of National Defense and Internal Affairs would remain in the hands of two communist generals, Florian Siwicki and Czesław Kiszczak, until July 1990. In his September 1989 parliamentary exposé, Tadeusz Mazowiecki somewhat misfortunately uttered a phrase that became a central (and thus far never-ending) source of public debate and—worst of all—social conflict. "We draw between the past and the present a thick line" ["Przeszłość odkreślamy grubą kreską"], said Mazowiecki in his address on August 24, 1989. While the goal was to make people focus on the current economic affairs, reject collective responsibility, and establish individual professional competence as the main criterion of the evaluation of public officials (Łazor & Morawski 2016), many interpretations of Mazowiecki's words would fail to recognize these intentions. Instead, for a large number of people—conservative politicians, journalists, and ordinary Poles—the "thick line" became a shameful symbol of general amnesty, a moral as well as judicial pardon granted to the main figures of the passing regime by their Round Table "accomplices."

These attitudes led to a major political crisis in 1992, under the rule of a manifestly anti-communist conservative government of Jan Olszewski. In May 1992 the government's Minister of Internal Affairs Antoni Macierewicz (who was, incidentally, to become a minister in the Law & Justice government in 2015) revealed the Ministry's information on the top politicians who had allegedly collaborated with the communist Secret Service before 1989. Containing sixty-four names of current parliamentarians as well as members of the former post-1989 governments, the list would raise strong doubts and controversies, many continuing until today. It was not obvious, for example, whether the sixty-four names on the list were those of actual security agents, or of the people on whom the Ministry had data, whether they were agents or agents' victims. Ironically, the list contained Lech Wałęsa, as well as many other prominent Solidarity members. Eventually, the crisis triggered by the publication led to the collapse of Olszewski's government, which lost a no-confidence vote in the parliament in June 1992. Interestingly, the vote was backed not only by the post-communist left, but also by a significant part of the post-Solidarity camp. In retrospect, the political split over Macierewicz's list can be considered reflection of a major divide emerging in the Polish sociopolitical space and public discourse in the 1990s. On the one hand, a significant part of the people and its parliamentary representation would call for "decommunization," a radical policy of removing from public positions all those whose records revealed any links to the apparatus of the communist state. These calls were supported by a non-negligible part of the media, including the right-wing newspaper *Gazeta Polska* and some of the nationwide TV channels such as TV Trwam. On the other hand, most people (at least until 2015) considered such a policy unreasonable and unjust, since under communist rule many people (even those in seemingly "unpolitical" jobs such as schoolteachers or public administration employees) would become part of the system automatically or without being aware of it (Łazor & Morawski 2016). Such a position is shared, until today, by the biggest Polish daily *Gazeta Wyborcza*, as well as other center and left-of-center media such as the TVN Group.

In the course of the years following the 1992 crisis, the divide over decommunization led to substantial radicalization of public discourse in Poland, fueling political attacks and mutual accusations on both sides of the barricade. The narratives developed in the two camps to communicate these attacks were equally threat-based. The right-wing conservative camp would frame decommunization as an urgent issue of national security, crucial for maintaining political independence from Russia. Consequently, within that frame all opponents of fast and unconditional decommunization were deemed to be "post-communists," "anti-nationals," or even "national traitors" (Gazeta Polska, May 4, 1999). On the other hand, the majority of Poland's political scene in the 1990s showed a restrained attitude toward radical decommunization, warning of "inconceivable social consequences of unprepared and inconsiderate actions" (Gazeta Wyborcza, July 16, 1998). At the same time, the supporters of such measures were presented as politically irresponsible and "playing out their own interests at the expense of the Polish people" (Gazeta Wyborcza, March 3, 1999). The gap only widened in the wake of the EU accession campaign in 2003. The conservative forces (such as the League of Polish Families, or even the newly created Law & Justice party) demonstrated a great deal of skepticism with regard to the accession, outlining possible disadvantages (of economic nature) or even dangers (such as sacrificing a significant part of national identity). This stance was in turn considered by the ruling liberal left as "a threat to Poland's security," in the sense that it created "a risk of exclusion from the civilized Europe for another 50 years" (PM Leszek Miller in Gazeta Wyborcza, June 3, 2003). The aura of ideological conflict in Polish sociopolitical space and public discourse would thus thicken, notwithstanding the positive result of the EU accession referendum in June 2004 (Krzyżanowski 2009).

From our bird's-eye perspective, the last big (and tragic) event stimulating social conflict in Poland before Law & Justice came to power was the Smolensk air disaster in spring 2010. On April 10, 2010, a Tupolev aircraft of the Polish Air Force crashed near the Russian city of Smolensk, killing all ninety-six people on board. Among the victims were the president of Poland Lech Kaczyński, his wife, as well as senior military officers, eighteen parliamentarians, and senior members of the Polish clergy. The group was arriving from Warsaw to attend an event commemorating the seventieth anniversary of the Katyń massacre,[4] which took place not far from Smolensk. Though victims of the crash came from all sides of the political spectrum, the majority (including the president) were associated with Law & Justice, which was then in opposition to the ruling Civic Platform party. Both the Russian and Polish official investigations found no technical faults with the aircraft, and concluded that the crew failed to conduct the approach in a safe manner in the given weather conditions. The Polish inquiry found also serious deficiencies in the organization and training of the air force unit involved, which was subsequently disbanded (Myslik et al. 2019).

Since the day of the accident various conspiracy theories have been in circulation, propagated mostly by Law & Justice politicians. They maintained that the crash was in fact a political assassination, an act of war against Poland or an elaborate coup attempt, possibly orchestrated by Russia. Law & Justice's leader and the president's brother Jarosław Kaczyński repeatedly accused the then-PM Donald Tusk of being "in some way" involved (Kaczyński in Gazeta Polska, April 3, 2011). The range of these accusations and of threatening conspiracy theories has been described by some international media as "dizzying"; from the idea that the fog around the airport had been artificially produced, to victims' bodies being doctored in fake autopsies, to the idea that explosives were planted on board the plane (Frankfurter Allgemeine Zeitung, October 11, 2012). Still, opinion polls in 2012 and 2013 found that one-third of Poles think it is possible that the Smolensk crash was an assassination. For eight years following the disaster, the area in front of the presidential palace in Warsaw became the venue of monthly public assemblies commemorating the victims, while at the same time "demanding truth" and accusing Tusk and his government of "covering up the real causes" of the tragedy. Over time, these assemblies would meet with numerous counterprotests demanding the end of the "Smolensk madness" (Myslik et al. 2019). In the media, the conservative and liberal news outlets, associated with Law & Justice and the Civic Platform, respectively, were fighting their own battle. In sum, as a result of this broad and multilevel conflict, Polish public sphere became further divided and polarized, providing fertile ground for populist, radical, and exclusionary discourses.

2.3. Poland in 2015: Internal and External Perspectives on the *Us*-and-*Them* Mindset and Public Discourse

We can see from this necessarily synthetic sketch that the postwar and, later, post-1989 history of Poland is a history of multiple political twists and turbulences, giving rise to divisions and conflicts triggering a significant polarization of public opinion. We can also see that Polish discourse has never been neutral to these developments, becoming a potent tool to promote as well as reject ideological visions and postures and, in the case of government leaders, to legitimize and perform state policies. Over years, all these enactments of discourse have come to rely on firmly entrenched conceptual oppositions and their rhetorical elaborations, particularly threat and fear generation patterns. Looking at the evolution of Polish public discourse in the past few decades, the present time sees perhaps the strongest articulations of the social divide ever, turning the *Us*-and-*Them* mindset into its increasingly distinctive *Them*-vs.-*Us* variation. The current levels of social polarization and radicalization of public discourse go back, arguably, to the year 2015, marking victories of the Law & Justice party in first the presidential and then the parliamentary elections. Given that in the entire postwar history of Poland and its political scene the right wing has only been in rule on two relatively brief occasions in 1992 and 2006, one must ask a question about the specific sociopolitical conditions which brought the Law & Justice conservatives to power in the fall of 2015. This begs some related questions as well, especially how the ongoing consolidation of the *Them*-vs.-*Us* mindset affected the 2015 campaign, and how the campaigners would play out these categories on different occasions and relative to different thematic issues and domains. Finally, there is an interesting question of whether the *Us*-and-*Them* and *Them*-vs.-*Us* mindsets have ever led to comparably momentous developments and changes anywhere else in Central Europe. That latter issue emerges as particularly intriguing given some common background and geopolitical similarities across the region (Popow 2015).

In general, the context of the 2015 campaign reflected most of the anxieties and fears that Polish people had accumulated after the 1989 transformation. These fears were swiftly bound up by Law & Justice political marketers with the most representative values and the central policymaking strategies of the then-ruling party, Civic Platform. First of all, there was an ever-growing fear of economic and social exclusion following what was considered an excessive attachment of the liberal government to "free market fundamentalism" and nearly "predatory" capitalism (Gazeta Polska, May 15, 2015), leaving behind those unable to adjust to the new economic reality after the transformation (Łazor & Morawski 2016). As this kind of anxiety was one of the most widespread social emotions experienced by Polish people after 1989, invoking it in the campaign allowed Law & Justice to secure unequivocal support of multiple social and professional groups who were in actuality of very different political predispositions and opinions. The support was thus earned in an essentially negative campaign, in which attacking the adversary was more frequent and more effective than presentation of own political proposals—except the proposals for direct social benefits such as "Family 500+".[5] In the course of the campaign, the liberal government became increasingly perceived as an ideological *Them*, ready to sacrifice the well-being of ordinary people to keep macroeconomic indicators intact. One of the most renowned Polish political scientists Radosław Markowski explained the situation in the following simple words:

> While Poland's overall economic health is strong, some groups and some parts of the country are suffering. Youth unemployment is twice the national average. Good jobs are scarce in small towns and rural regions, especially in eastern Poland. Many people are working under short-term contracts that carry few protections or benefits. And although Poland was the only country in the EU to avoid a recession after the post-2008 global crisis, that came at a cost: The government imposed austerity measures (including pay freezes for some public employees), while private businesses often imposed pay cuts while simultaneously demanding higher productivity. (Markowski in The Washington Post, November 3, 2015)

In the Law & Justice's 2015 campaign narrative, the construction of *Them* involved also identification of numerous external threats and attributing their growth to apparent inaction of the government. Here, the 2015 migrant crisis in Europe emerged as a huge political and rhetorical asset. Arguing adamantly against the EU proposal for a quota system to deliver a certain percentage of migrants to each country, Law & Justice deemed the government's acceptance of the proposal an act of national betrayal. During the entire campaign, its leaders stoked fears that the refugees and migrants would threaten Poland's national security, religious and cultural identity, economic well-being, and even public health (Łazor & Morawski 2016). This narrative led with time to conceptual conflation and otherization of the migrants and government liberals, placing both in a common *Them* camp.

Finally, throughout the campaign leaders of Law & Justice were able to induce anxieties of geopolitical nature, which had been dormant in Polish people for much longer than the post-1989 transformation period. This involved reactivation of fears associated with Poland's historical geopolitical vulnerability to the ambitions of its more powerful neighbors: Germany and Russia. We have observed earlier in the present chapter that the vision of "German threat" persisted in Poland for decades after the Second World War, virtually until today. At the same time, anti-Russian sentiment developed considerably as a result of the Soviet political control over countries of the Eastern bloc in the Cold War period. In the campaign, Law & Justice leaders were able to readdress these anxieties and phobias and redefine them according to the current international context. Thus, a prominent place in the campaign was given to the Russian-German Nord Stream project,[6] which was presented as a major growing threat to Polish economy and, consequently, Poland's political sovereignty (Gazeta Polska, December 4, 2009). As will be shown in the following chapters, this issue remained an integral part of the Law & Justice discourse after the elections as well. Simultaneously, the distrustful attitude of Polish people to the country's neighbors was used consistently in the service of criticism of the liberal government. Thus, Donald Tusk and his ministers were reproached for being too soft on the Russian and German economic expansion (Łazor & Morawski 2016). These critical opinions were followed, after 2010, by massive criticism and outright accusations of Tusk's negligence with respect to the Russian inquiry into reasons for the Smolensk air disaster. As in the case of the migrant and refugee crisis a few years later, the alleged inaction of the Polish government was deemed by Law & Justice a betrayal of Poland's raison d'état. All these claims and accusations fell on fertile ground during the 2015 campaign, making a significant contribution to Law & Justice's victory (Gazeta Wyborcza, November 2, 2015).

From a broader geopolitical perspective, the rise of populism and the polarization of political attitudes and public discourse that occurred in Poland after 1989 and, further, in the years preceding the 2015 elections are not phenomena alien to other countries of the former Soviet bloc (Cordell and Jajecznik 2015). The long-awaited "return to Europe" of Central European countries in 1989 entailed two parallel and complementary transitions: the reclamation of a Western democratic identity and a conversion to liberalism. Eager to merge with the West (politically and mentally), the people in Central Europe were ready to embrace both of these transitions unequivocally and fast. Their governments would for a long time side with European giants such as Germany and France on the vast majority of political issues and specific policies, including some controversial measures such as the EU economic policies imposed on Greece and other Southern European countries during the financial crisis in 2008. That pro-European stance has nonetheless changed significantly with the rise of populist forces throughout Europe— the AfD in Germany, the National Front in France, Bepe Grillo's Movimento Cinque Stelle in Italy, the FPÖ in Austria, or Geert Wilders in Holland. It is believed (Cordell and Jajecznik 2015) that the example set by these forces exerted a substantial influence on the countries of Central Europe, leading to a certain—and apparently premature—"democracy fatigue." The latter would manifest itself in the departure from the rule of law as the foundation of liberal democracy as represented by European institutions in the name of the so-called "sovereignty of the people," the repatriation of powers to the nation-states. The most extreme example of such a shift has been arguably Hungary, where, "following the popular will," PM Viktor Orban and his national-conservative Fidesz party brought back to life some judicial institutions and administrative regulations associated with the former communist dictatorship. These anti-democratic and anti-European changes in Hungary in the last decade produced a massive sociopolitical divide, leading to the emergence of new radical discourses (Schmölz 2019). There are also other recent examples of discursive populism and radicalism grounded in social polarization across Central Europe, from the anti-migration stance and increasingly anti-European discourse of members of the Visegrád Group (Schmölz 2019), to lenient reactions from the governments of Romania and Bulgaria to acts of public discrimination of the Roma population (Nicolae 2013). The number of such examples in the Central European public discourse is, unfortunately, growing.

2.4. Mapping the Law & Justice Discourse: Domains, Themes, and the Text Corpus

Notwithstanding these similarities as well as analogies to other far-right discourses around Europe, the rhetoric of Law & Justice remains a genuinely exceptional example of populist conservative discourse. Its uniqueness involves a number of factors and interrelated features that make a joint contribution to the effectiveness of this rhetoric as a means of social coercion and policy legitimization. First, the crisis construction, threat generation, and fear management that underlie the Law & Justice discourse extend over a great number of domains, from international relations to local matters of healthcare or education. The fear appeals and threat-based argumentation patterns occurring in these domains are often mutually related, enhancing consistency of the global message. For example, recent attempts to legitimize regulations restricting judges' freedom to comment on the ongoing judicial reform typically take place at two levels. At the home level, the new regulations are presented as tough, but necessary, measures to offset what Law & Justice legislators call "anarchy threat," posed by judges' reluctance to accept sweeping changes imposing political control over the judiciary. Simultaneously, at international level, defense of these regulations (at the European Parliament and the European Court of Justice) is perceived in terms of the national raison d'état, and all attempts to oppose the new laws are deemed a sovereignty threat.

Furthermore, the very special thing about the Law & Justice discourse is that for the past five years leaders of the party (and Jarosław Kaczyński in particular) have been using its threat-based coercive powers not only to respond to objectively occurring crisis situations but also to provoke different conflicts and crises themselves, in order to propose ready-made "solutions" and thus strengthen their leadership. Law & Justice emerges in these efforts as close followers of some of the old (and not always noble) traditions of the Polish political propaganda. We have seen in this chapter how the artificially generated threat of the Colorado beetle was helpful to communist propagandists in their attempts to trigger social mobilization and translate people's anger into increased motivation to work. Nowadays, strikingly similar strategies of inventing virtual threats are followed by Law & Justice leaders, such as the outrageous, pseudo-scientific argument that Middle East refugees may be carrying "a special type of bacteria," which Kaczyński once made to support his party's anti-migration stance. Another historical case in which political crisis was provoked internally to facilitate enactment of government's policies was the publication of a list of security agents by Antoni Macierewicz in the 1990s, which we discussed in the previous section. That case can in turn be compared with the 2017 publication of selected secret files stored in the Institute of National Remembrance, containing information on the former Solidarity leaders. Though according to the government the opening of the archives took place in the interest of "general transparency of public life," it is believed (Gazeta Wyborcza, May 4, 2017) that the underlying reason was to discredit Lech Wałęsa, known for his blatant criticism of Kaczyński and other top party figures. Altogether, while the attachment of Law & Justice to past political traditions and behaviors is often nothing to take pride on, one cannot deny Kaczyński's historical sensitiveness, political intuition, and mainly the ability to recontextualize old practices and discourses precisely in the service of current goals. This ability makes for another reason that sets the Law & Justice discourse apart from other far-right populist discourses in Europe—despite the similarities.

In the next four chapters we conduct a text study of discourse of the Law & Justice party in the course of its full parliamentary term 2015–19, from the conspicuous victory in the October 2015 elections to the last moments preceding the October 2019 election battle—again victorious for the ruling party. The analyzed corpus[7] includes 500 speeches, statements, comments, and remarks by the most prominent and influential of Law & Justice politicians: Prime Ministers Beata Szydło (2015–17) and Mateusz Morawiecki (2017–19), representatives of the most important ministries, the Law & Justice party leader Jarosław Kaczyński and his MPs. It also includes speeches from the same period by the President of Poland Andrzej Duda, supported by Law & Justice in his 2015 campaign, and in the current campaign for the upcoming May 2020 elections. In Chapters 3 and 4 we focus on home issues—"decommunization," post-1989 divisions, economic inequality, discrimination, social exclusion, and ideological conflict—emerging in national/local discourse domains such as parliamentary sessions, rallies, or interviews with the media. In Chapters 5 and 6 the focus is on the Law & Justice discourse of international relations, including cooperation with(in) the European Union as well as relations with Russia and Germany. Throughout the analysis, several analogies will be drawn to far-right discourses in other European countries (Hungary, Romania, Bulgaria, Italy, and the UK), with regard to dominant themes (European [dis-]integration, multiculturalism, migration, welfare state) and the main structural and pragmatic features.

3

Enemy at Home

"Total Opposition," "Post-Communist Elites," and "Keepers of the Round Table Order"

The previous chapter has shown that crisis construction, conflict generation, and threat management have long been an integral element of Polish politics and public policy, defining the stance of numerous legitimization and coercive discourses in virtually all areas of public life. Building on this tradition in the 2015 campaign, Law & Justice leaders were able to recontextualize the old practices and discourses in the service of current goals. The result was an apparently surprising, yet convincing, victory in both presidential and parliamentary elections. Interestingly, the subsequent discourse of Law & Justice has changed little compared to the campaign rhetoric. Indeed, the discourse of Law & Justice as a ruling party is still a deeply coercive discourse, keeping threat and fear levels at a continual high.

This chapter and the next explore the discourse of Law & Justice (henceforth: L&J) on the home arena. In the present chapter we focus on the discourse directed at L&J's opposition in the Polish parliament (in its 2015–19 term). This includes statements and remarks made directly *to* the opposition MPs at parliamentary sessions, as well as public and media comments *about* the opposition in general. Most of these comments concern the Civic Platform party (henceforth: CP), which ruled Poland in the years 2007–15, to become the main oppositional force after the 2015 elections.

The discussion in the chapter demonstrates that L&J's home-front discourse makes a consistent use of pragmatic distancing strategies to situate the opposition, in conceptual terms, at the remotest end of the *Us/Them* spectrum. Specifically, it conflates the CP and its followers with post-communist groups and ex-leaders of the country (referred to as "post-communist elites"), by presenting CP politicians as "keepers of the Round Table order."[1] That way, it construes the opposition as unfaithful to "core values" and "vital interests" of the people. The result is a firm *othering* arrangement, whereby the opposition is conceptualized as a symbolic *Them* entity threatening the well-being of the *Us* entity ("real Poles") under the current leadership. The enactment of this arrangement involves a spectrum of judgments and negative images, such as selling Polish property to foreign investors by the former CP government, inability to handle unemployment and economic migration from Poland, promoting multiculturalism at the expense of Polish cultural and religious heritage, incorporating non-Polish liberal values into family life, and many others.

On a text-analytical plane, the chapter shows how these conceptualizations are performed by linguistic means, especially the STATE IS HOME, NATION IS BODY, and POLITICS IS WAR metaphoric scenarios, as well as deixis of proximity and distance. At the same time, it reveals how the aura of conflict and crisis is perpetuated by the application of proximization. In particular, proximization strategies are shown to produce fear appeals that induce acceptance of L&J's leadership as the only way to avoid return of the Round Table order and then, likely, a (post-)communist rule. In its final part, the chapter explores the existence of similar (and different) strategies in other European discourses, such as the discourse of Viktor Orban's leadership in Hungary, as well as discourses of the League and the Five Star Movement during the 2018 government formation in Italy.

3.1. "In the Past Eight Years. . ."

We have observed in the previous chapter that L&J's victory in the 2015 elections was due, in many ways, to its ability to address the anxieties and fears that Polish people had accumulated after the 1989 transformation, such as the fear of economic and social exclusion in the new reality of liberal rule and free market capitalism. In the course of the campaign, one of the main strategies was to show the indifference of the CP government to significant social costs that had to be paid for the health of the global economy: youth unemployment in eastern regions of Poland, scarcity of good jobs in smaller towns, work on short-term contracts carrying few or no benefits, closures of small factories, and the like. While Poland in 2015 was looking back on more than a decade of unbroken economic growth, with joblessness in fact the lowest that anyone had seen since 1989, social insecurity, a poor small-business climate, and unsatisfactory public services (especially healthcare) remained serious irritants. Building on these issues, Law & Justice managed to integrate the often contradictory discontents of different social groups into a deeply counterfactual "Poland in ruins" narrative, wherein L&J pledged to "rebuild" Poland after the devastation allegedly wrought by CP's eight-year rule, or even the quarter-century of Poland's democratic transformation. L&J's continued attachment to this narrative in the campaign produced, at places, some absurd situations. A few weeks before the elections, the then-candidate for Prime Minister, Beata Szydło, staged a press conference in a ruined factory building in a provincial town to prove her point. Outraged, the town's mayor (a CP politician) summoned the media to show that his town was actually booming, and even the derelict factory was in for a revamp. But that was, eventually, to little avail: many of the public only had ears for the populist message of doom.

Remarkably, the "Poland in ruins" narrative did not end after the 2015 elections, but continues, in an updated form, over the entire 2015–19 parliamentary term. The updated narrative includes, apart from the election promise to "rebuild" Poland, a number of fear appeals involving historical flashbacks. The most frequent appeal presupposes the threat of a possible return of the ultra-liberal and socially ruthless rule, which is simultaneously construed as the only alternative to the L&J rule. In this way, the discourse of Law & Justice defines and perpetuates a cleavage between two (and only two) political mindsets: one that involves a sense of individual security resulting from pro-social policy of the state, and the other, antagonistic mindset. The latter is attributed, directly, to the parliamentary opposition, but potentially to anyone who the ruling party deems a political or economic beneficiary of the post-1989 period. The outlines of this divide emerge from Kaczyński's victory speech on the October 25 election night, in which he establishes security as a dominant concept of his party governance:

(1) Our mandate to rule is defined by our commitment to security. This includes external security, internal security, which in the modern state is especially social security, as well as commercial and economic security.

> Finally, the security that every state must provide to its citizens as it guarantees to itself. The state is also a dispenser of goods. And all of these processes which are associated with the use of state power for the distribution of goods may deviate to a form of pathology and can lead to various kinds of abuse. That is why we have to treat that last type of security very seriously. I think we can say that what Poles expect today from the state is security, freedom, equality, and justice, which in Poland is always linked with solidarity. These are particularly important expectations. (Jarosław Kaczyński, election night address, October 25, 2015)

The text in (1) may not look particularly expressive, yet it possesses a number of distinctive features which make up a framework for later rhetoric. First, it defines priorities of the new government, and the central concepts of governance, such as "security," "freedom," "equality," and "justice." The concept that is addressed most frequently, security, reveals a substantial rhetorical velocity, the capacity for discursive recontextualization and sharing. As has been discussed in Chapter 1, the velocity feature allows for the message to get recomposed and redistributed by its original recipients, which broadens the target range of the audience. This is because the recipients find the shared message positive or reassuring, and apparently beneficial to themselves. The concept of security is an excellent candidate for discursive recirculation, as it reveals an unequivocally positive appeal to large numbers of people. As such, it is also a viable premise on which to build further, potentially more controversial messages and argumentation patterns. We have seen from the first chapter that such patterns often need a long preparatory sequence before they can be communicated successfully and the success depends on each and every element of the sequence falling within the "latitude of acceptance" of the addressee (cf. 1.3). The concept of security fits into such preparatory sequences exceptionally well.

The conceptual framework of security and individual safety enacted in (1) is also a vital prerequisite for the effectiveness of conflict, crisis, and fear rhetoric in later discourse. The moment (a sense of) security is established, it is exposed to assault and destruction. Thus, in rhetorical terms, it sanctions a threat-based coercive discourse, which defines the source of the threat and proposes preemptive or preventive action. Although text (1) is still relatively scarce in direct fear appeals, it includes, in the area of economy and social policy, as well as state governance in general, indications of an antagonistic mindset, which leads to "pathology" and "abuse." There is, so far, no attribution of these concepts to a specific political entity, but we will see that it takes Kaczyński and L&J only a couple of months to use them quite regularly as ideological tags on the oppositional party and their rule before the elections. Incidentally, the vagueness of reference and a tendency for impersonalization (especially in respect to political *Them*) emerge, already at this point, as a distinctive feature of Kaczyński's rhetorical idiolect (Bunikowski 2018).

Finally, text (1) construes security in its enactment of common ground, a sense of public participation in the pursuit of common goal. Invoking the notion of "solidarity" and acknowledging the awareness of people's "expectations," Kaczyński starts to draw another important distinction between L&J and the outgoing CP rule. The key element of this mapping, the concept of government that stays close to its people, is to remain a core feature of L&J's discourse until today. In many texts, it serves to create a stark contrast with the opposition, creating the aura of lasting ideological conflict, whose roots go back to the 1989 transformation. This is done to construe the CP camp as direct heirs and main beneficiaries of the Round Table compromise:

(2) If you look at the past 8 years, and in fact the past 27 years we had to deal with the overwhelming predominance of one group. In the area of ownership, media, and also in the public life for the vast majority of the time, in these 27 years. The establishment in this country said that everything was OK. But everything was not OK. Conditions to develop the rule of law arose only today, as we are able to rebuild it, or actually create it, because in Poland for a very long time there was no right balance. The elites of the old communist regime switched into the new system, maintaining their advantage, transforming and exchanging power for property. The prevalence of that group continues to be felt in the realm of the mass media, in the economy, of course, and in various state institutions, for example the judiciary, which was so favorable to the previous government. And this is what we want to fix, to change, step by step. We must try to consolidate Polish society at large along the lines of positive Polish traditions and values, to oppose what I call the "pedagogy of shame," the tendency that has dominated Poland over the past 8 years. We need new policy in terms of education, in terms of culture. This is not revolution but reform. But, by the very nature of change, it will result in conflict. (Jarosław Kaczyński, parliamentary speech, January 21, 2016)

While this parliamentary address comes only three months after the election night speech, its message is far more pronounced in deictic and performative terms. Assessing the effects of the past twenty-seven years of Poland's political and economic transformation, Kaczyński points to specific areas of negligence ("rule of law"), identifies reasons and the social and political groups responsible ("elites of the old communist regime"), and finally proposes new policies ("in terms of education, in terms of culture"). Text (2) can thus be read as a follow-up on text (1) in that it develops abstract and essentially tone-setting concepts of governance such as equality, security, freedom, or justice, into concrete solutions and action plans. The analyzed corpus data warrants an observation that such a combination of tone-setting and policy-setting speeches (or textual segments within a speech) is a distinctive feature of L&J's discourse in the entire 2015–19 term. However, as the term goes on, the policy-setting element becomes more and more salient, and policies are presented mostly as means to offset a specific economic or social threat. All this reveals substantial consistency of L&J's discourse at the macro-level of enactment of political credibility and leadership. In line with the classic principles of homeostasis (cf. 1.3), Kaczyński and other L&J speakers are careful to precede any potentially controversial messages with assertions of abstract yet indisputable truths.

In functional terms, the speech in (2) realizes a pattern of conceptual conflation, whereby the political camp of the Civic Platform is linked to "the old communist regime" through the participation in the Round Table arrangements (though the Round Table as such is not mentioned in the text). This is again a rhetorical characteristic which pertains to L&J's discourse and its stance on the opposition in the whole term. In (2), the conflation involves seeing both "power" and "property" as valuable commodities that can be mutually exchanged or traded. As a result, the conceptualization of Civic Platform as a liberal party supporting market economy and privatization meets the conceptualization of "communist elites," construing one complex image of political-economic establishment wielding their power and influence over decades, now in new capitalist, modern disguises.

Given the caliber of oppression suffered by Polish people during communist years (cf. Chapter 2), such a construal situates the opposition, mostly composed of CP members and followers, at the very remote end of the *Us/Them* (or *Them* vs. *Us*) spectrum. The positioning of CP as an ideological *Them* involves, further, the conceptualization of CP rule as a period of Poland's sociopolitical dependency and cultural subordination. This conceptualization lies implicit in the "pedagogy of shame," one of the most frequent phrases in Kaczyński's discourse.[2] Coined in spring 2007, it has been used to denote a kind of sociopolitical inferiority complex characterizing, in Kaczyński's opinion, the CP government, mostly in the area of foreign policy and relations with the European Union in particular (Hayden 2018). In his speech in (2), Kaczyński does not feel he needs to explain or elaborate on the phrase, assuming—rightly—its substantial popularity. Instead, he goes on to realize the most important function of the entire speech—the declaration of a crisis situation. Meticulously developed in the course of the text, the assertion of "conflict" in the final line comes as a natural and politically responsible judgment based on rational assessment of the *Them* and *Us* ideological standpoints that cannot be reconciled. This is another example of how the text follows the principles of psychological and rhetorical consistency.

In the course of the parliamentary term 2015–19, the most conspicuous features of Kaczyński's discourse show up, increasingly often, in speeches of other prominent L&J politicians. This includes the stance on the opposition and, more generally, the social and economic divide for which, according to Law & Justice, the opposition is responsible. Among L&J leaders, Beata Szydło (the 2015–17 Prime Minister) emerges as one of the closest followers of Kaczyński's rhetorical style. Her parliamentary address on June 8, 2016, is a good example:

(3) In Poland we still have a sort of entire archipelago of small kingdoms and principalities, small dictatorships in municipalities, in factories, in universities. There, people are simply afraid. They are afraid to criticize and to have other opinions. For this we cannot agree. We need to eliminate this archipelago. I will say even more. Poland should be an island of freedom, even if everywhere else it will be limited. We were once an island of tolerance in Europe, and now we should become an island of freedom. And we need not be ashamed. This is our banner and great asset. This is our moral strength. This is not always so with equality and justice. Still lingers in Poland a kind of rule or principal, that Donald Tusk tried to impose on us in Poland. It divided Poles into two categories in which some people have the right to rule, while others do not. Because they wear mohair berets. (Beata Szydło, parliamentary speech, June 8, 2016)

Looking at (3), all the main ingredients of Kaczyński's discourse are there. The *Us* and *Them* distinction is intact, drawing upon the same kind of ideological conflict as in (2) the insurmountable difference between "those who are morally equipped to lead" (the L&J camp) and "those who agree to be led [in Europe]" (the CP camp, here symbolized by its ex-leader Donald Tusk). In Szydło's text, this conflict is construed to occur in yet another dimension, between the people and the local government, the latter still dominated by the liberals. The local government is thus referred to as an "entire archipelago" of "kingdoms," "principalities," and "dictatorships," which invokes the memory of not just the "27 years of post-communism," in Kaczyński's terms, but also of the communist rule before 1989. The appeal of this judgment is substantially enhanced by the use of conceptual metaphor ("archipelago"), which not only is rhetorically attractive and easily shareable but also initiates a narrative scenario of a widespread and developing threat that necessitates the use of specific measures (we discuss these coercive and legitimization powers of metaphor in the next section).

Similar to Kaczyński, Szydło construes the current conservative leadership as essentially pro-social, focused on the needs of ordinary, often elderly and poor people who, according to L&J, have been given no chance by CP liberals to benefit from Poland's economic growth following the transformation. At the end of the text, she refers to this group as "mohair berets," which involves a rhetorical trick, and in fact a manipulation. The phrase "mohair berets" was originally used in 2004 in the *Rzeczpospolita* newspaper article "Labyrinths of the Parish Priest" by Maja Narbutt (Rzeczpospolita, May 18, 2004), to describe the "old ladies" (hence the reference to a characteristic piece of headgear) that "have their eyes fixed on Father Jankowski," an outstanding church dignitary supporting the Solidarity movement in the 1980. Later, though, it developed a somewhat ironic meaning, denoting "a crowd of poor, elderly, devout women demonstrating their zealous support for the Polish conservative-nationalistic Catholic movement" (Novikova 2017). During Father Jankowski's funeral in July 2010, the then-leader of the Civic Platform Donald Tusk used the phrase in its original positive sense, provoking however a massive critique and attacks from right-wing commentators. In the conservative paper *Gazeta Polska* Tusk was accused of "insulting ordinary Poles" and "dismantling the ideological and religious framework of the nation" (Gazeta Polska, July 25, 2010). The inclusion of "mohair berets" by Szydło in her address in (3) is equally manipulative.

Drawing on textual proximity—the mention of Tusk in a previous sentence—it brings back the memory of his "scandalous use" of the phrase back in 2010, while simultaneously hiding the original interpretation.

In the second half of the 2015–19 period, the narrative of the CP rule and the conceptualization of the opposition in general changes. In the new, increasingly metaphoric narrative, the past "elites" are clearly on the defensive, yet still able to strike back:

> **(4)** Today, the great work of patriotic communities is bearing fruits. The assault on our Polish house is losing ground. The assault of putting to shame everything that is Polish, all this offensive, which undermines our community values, our national values, fortunately this assault is losing ground. Good is again separated from evil. Everything that was done to confuse good and evil, is now dwindling. We can say that a great white-red movement has been created. And this is what Poland needs. But the change is not yet complete. We must keep this in mind. We must remain vigilant. (Mateusz Morawiecki, PM's exposé, December 12, 2017)

Text (4) is an excerpt from a parliamentary exposé by Mateusz Morawiecki, thus far a finance minister, who replaced Beata Szydło as Prime Minister in December 2017. Morawiecki's nomination was part of the plan to refresh the image of the L&J government and to define new economic priorities, such as increased investment in skills and education, and technological development based on sustainability. The aim was, at the same time, to acknowledge the progress already made, creating a sense of national pride and that way facilitating the approval of future policy. These ideas are indeed salient in the text, which attributes the success ("bearing fruits") to the steadfastness of purpose, patriotic team spirit ("a great white-red movement") and, above all, the unfaltering commitment to Polish "national values." Such an argument is, in conceptual terms, a response to Kaczyński's call to do away with the "pedagogy of shame" underlying the CP rule, but also the introduction to a new kind of discourse characteristic of the years 2018–19. Over that period, L&J's parliamentary rhetoric gets increasingly threat-based and coercive, soliciting legitimization of public policies presented as necessary measures to protect the accomplishments of L&J's rule against a possible return of the liberals. At the textual level, this means a significant radicalization of language, involving the use of specific lexical forms construing various scenarios of external attack and defense. Some of these forms occur in Morawiecki's exposé text, such as "assault," "offensive," and, in particular, the lexical items associated with the HOUSE metaphor ("Polish house"). The use of the HOUSE metaphor in (4) serves, in its simplest interpretation, to enact a sense of internal security and a common commitment to its protection against a possible intrusion. However, there are also other, less obvious functions of this metaphor, as well as other metaphoric scenarios and conceptualizations as a whole that make a significant contribution to L&J's rhetoric in the final two years of the term. We discuss them next.

3.2. Metaphor Scenarios

The conspicuous turn to metaphorization in the 2018–19 period can be read as L&J's attempt to make their rhetoric more intense and emotional, with a view to strengthening its coercive appeal. This attempt involves concretizing the adversary and thus numerous metaphoric mappings are used to define the opposing positions of political entities within the ideological spectrum and relative to such basic concepts as "nation," "home," "ally," "enemy," and finally "war," marking a clash of opposing political visions. As a result, the *Us* and *Them* camps become further demarcated, facilitating the construal of threat to home entities from their adversaries. In general, metaphoric discourse of Law & Justice rests on the interplay of three conceptual scenarios. Allowing for some synonymity of the domains involved, these main scenarios can be expressed as follows: () POLITICS/POLITICAL CONFLICT IS WAR, (B) STATE IS HOME/BODY/PERSON, and (C) NATION/STATE/GOVERNMENT IS TEAM. As can be seen from this designation, the B–C scenarios are responsible for the mechanisms of conceptual inclusion, that is, in sociopolitical terms, the enactment of national unity and solidarity. As such, they also partake in the processes of othering and exclusion, in that they leave out the entities (individuals or groups) that are taken as opponents to the ideology associated with the STATE and NATION conceptual domains. This feature makes the B and C scenarios valuable elements of L&J's discourse, especially as regards its stance on the opposition, which is construed symbolically as alien to the cultural and ideological space within the STATE and NATION domains. However, in order for the B and C scenarios to function, the entities left out must be presented as genuinely antagonistic and capable of political encroachment or invasion. Hence the need for the A scenario, construing political conflict and politics generally in terms of war. The A scenario performs thus an essential coordinating function, embedding the *Us*-and-*Them* conflict in a potentially dramatic context. This function entails, at the linguistic level, a huge presence of relevant lexical forms, that is, items derived from the military domain. Here is an overview of the most numerous of such items[3] in the corpus (Table 3.1). The numbers are provided in total, as well as separately for the 2015–17 and 2017–19 periods. This is to elucidate the increased role of metaphorization in the second part of the term.

Table 3.1 includes fourteen most frequent items, each of which appears over 100 times in the L&J corpus. Of these fourteen items, eleven appear more frequently between October 2017 and September 2019 than between October 2015 and September 2017, even though the number of texts and the total number of words in the two periods are comparable. In the case of some items, differences between the two periods are quite staggering. This concerns the generally most frequent items, such as "to attack," "battle," "fight," and "to fight," representing the most direct attributes of WAR. The steep increase in the number of these items within the 2017–19 period reveals both the overall

Table 3.1 The Most Frequent Lexical Items of the WAR Source Domain in the POLITICS/POLITICAL CONFLICT IS WAR Metaphor

Item	October 2015–September 2017 (265 texts)	October 2017–September 2019 (235 texts)	Total of 500 texts
"to attack" ["atakować"]	201	443	644
"battle" ["bitwa"]	190	322	512
"fight" ["walka"]	194	291	485
"to fight" ["walczyć"]	116	311	427
"to defend" ["bronić"]	96	105	201
"strategy" ["strategia"]	112	68	180
"weapon" ["broń"]	53	124	177
"to clash" ["ścierać się"]	85	56	141
"army" ["armia"]	55	81	136
"to win" ["zwyciężyć"]	65	65	130
"team" ["drużyna"]	65	60	125
"to wage war" ["toczyć wojnę"]	36	74	110
"offensive" ["ofensywa"]	36	71	107
"battlefield" ["pole bitwy"]	35	67	102

increase in metaphoric discourse of the L&J party at the end of the parliamentary term and a significant radicalization of that discourse. By comparison, lexical items such as "strategy" and "clash" prevail in the 2015–17 period, indicating L&J's ideological visions and policy plans ("strategy"), as well as awareness of a possible conflict ("clash") resulting from enactment of these plans and visions. Such abstract construals become pragmatically ineffective in the later period, hence the switch to emotionally appealing language forms triggering more coercive conceptualizations.

Although the role and frequency of metaphor and metaphoric scenarios grow as the parliamentary term goes on, a conspicuous start is made relatively early—in Jarosław Kaczyński's speech in front of the Constitutional Tribunal on December 13, 2015.[4] The metaphoric constructions used in that speech provide a blueprint for later rhetoric:

(5) The opposition says "we are defending$_A$ democracy against dictatorship." But what kind of a defense$_A$ is it? The opposition will act without any limits, it will attack$_A$ the government, it will attack$_A$ the president. As I speak, they are setting out their forces, digging trenches, positioning the army$_A$. They are trying to convince people that in the middle of a hot summer it is a freezing, harsh winter. And there are people who will hear something on TVN—this industry of contempt—and be ready to believe it. They will go outside, dress in a winter coat, and still say that they are cold. But these are not people who are right in the head, who think correctly. Right here are the people who think, and who know perfectly well that in Poland there is no threat to democracy. And you can count on us, the red and white team$_C$, we will manage. We will all manage and win$_C$. (. . .) This is mostly about fear. About ensuring that the gigantic wave of abuse that took place over the past eight years does not come to light. Those who, during the so-called transformation, abandoned communism, gave up power for property—they want to continue to get fat. Right here among us, under our roof$_B$. And those who were coopted into that group, too. But their room for manoeuver$_A$ is shrinking. The Constitutional Tribunal was supposed to be their last defense$_A$. For yesterday's rulers and today's opposition. For everything that was bad and disgraceful over the past 26 years. For every disease and pathology this country was infested with$_B$. And we want to change that. And therefore we must change the Tribunal. We must make it into an institution that will truly be for the citizens, that will defend the constitution, but not in a way that allows the constitution to apply to some but not others. And we must do it quickly. Otherwise we'll forever get stuck in the trenches dug$_A$ by

Schetyna and his party. That's the true meaning of today's underline{battle}~A~. (Jarosław Kaczyński, December 13, 2015)

In (5), the underlined words and phrases are lexicalizations of metaphoric construals in general, and the subscripts mark the items realizing the particular scenarios: (A) POLITICS/POLITICAL CONFLICT IS WAR, (B) STATE IS HOME/BODY/PERSON, and (C) NATION/STATE/GOVERNMENT IS TEAM. The prevalence of items enacting the (A) scenario is well visible, proving a key role of the scenario in forcing the remaining conceptualizations. As will be seen in later examples, the central lexicalizations of the (A) scenario, "attack," "defend," and "battle" (as well as "fight," missing in [5]) are there to stay for the entire term, getting even more frequent and appealing in the 2017–19 period. Altogether, the (A) scenario performs a crucial function of *contextualization* of actions and states of affairs predicated in the (B) and (C) scenarios. Specifically, it legitimizes the exclusion from the *Us* camp of the entities and forces declaring themselves as political opponents to *Us* entities. This is because the scenario turns political conflict and politics in general into a conceptual phenomenon that involves mutual hostility and expectations of a material conflict, thus sanctioning actions to keep the potential invader off the home territory. Indications of such an impending clash are plentiful throughout the text, which defines the enemy ("Schetyna and his party"[5]), the gathering threat ("they are setting out their forces. . ."), and possible consequences of ignoring that threat ("we'll forever get stuck in the trenches. . ."). Regarding the latter, the metaphor of "trenches" "dug" by the opposition is to gain further popularity in the years 2017–19, playing an extra role of justifying the unfulfillment of some of the 2015 election promises.

From the perspective of state leadership and policymaking, the POLITICS/POLITICAL CONFLICT IS WAR scenario realized in (5) reveals some excellent pragmatic qualities. As a pattern of understanding based on universal experience (cf. 1.4.2), it furthers a default assessment of the presented state of affairs and legitimizes a default set of actions or solutions associated with it. Since, in a war context, invasion entails response, a similar general mechanism guides a political conflict. Thus, calls for policies such as "we must change the Tribunal" earn their credibility and legitimacy quite automatically. What is more, the automaticity of understanding and behavior associated with the scenario ensures its quick uptake and recirculation. In other words, the actions and solutions presented by the original political actor—the L&J party—are likely to get further propagated by members of the political audience. The speech in (5) includes some extra ploys that facilitate this process, for instance, deixis of person ("we") is often used in nominal phrases that announce actions and policies (as in "we must make it into an institution that. . ."). Naturally enough, another function of such markers is the enactment of common obligation and responsibility, which is a standard feature of L&J discourse.[6]

Assisted by the (A) scenario, the (B) and (C) mappings consolidate the *Us* camp and unite its members in a joint course of action. These two functions are realized, respectively, by the STATE IS HOME/BODY/PERSON and NATION/STATE/GOVERNMENT IS TEAM scenarios. In addition, the (B) STATE IS HOME/BODY/PERSON scenario plays an important role in legitimizing the actions prescribed by the other, (C) NATION/STATE/GOVERNMENT IS TEAM scenario. Specifically, the construal of STATE in terms of HOME, BODY, or PERSON allows a quick and unequivocal justification of response to an alleged threat to entities subsumed by the STATE concept. In text (5) this response involves, at the lexico-grammatical level, ridding the "country" of the "disease and pathology" that has been spreading "under [its] roof" for the "past 26 years." Such a reaction is not only morally justified but also easy to understand and natural. This is because the source domain of the scenario involves, apart from the HOME concept, also the BODY and PERSON concepts. As such, the scenario makes it possible to consider policies of the STATE in metaphoric terms of restoring the state's health.

The speech in (5) is the earliest in the L&J corpus where the STATE IS BODY metaphor is used for the purpose of moral justification and policy legitimization. However, over the 2015–19 period the L&J discourse includes gradually more and more forms and expressions where Poland is conceptualized as a country "infected" by all kinds of ideological, political or cultural diseases, be them the "unpatriotic opposition," post-communists, extreme leftists ["lewacy"], or environmentalists, feminists, and LGBT groups. Arguably, one reason for the popularity (and rhetorical effectiveness) of the conceptualization of POLAND in terms of BODY is a similarity of this mapping to the POLAND IS PERSON metaphor, which has a particularly long history in Polish public discourse (Gomola 2019). We have noted in the previous chapter that already in the 120-year-long period of lost independence Polish literature would liken Poland to the "Messiah of nations," viewing the country's suffering as redeeming of the world's ills. As observed by Gomola

(2019: 84–5), that romantic tradition led over time to the creation of several metonymic elaborations, all religious in nature, such as "Poland is a defender of the Catholic faith" or "Poland is a missionary for Europe." Perhaps the most extreme of these elaborations appeared after the Smolensk air disaster in 2010, drawing parallels between the crash of the presidential plane and Christ's crucifixion:

> **(6)** Such a tragedy—in a certain sense the greatest one on the global scale—cannot be unrelated directly and radically to Christ's sacrifice. More than that, it is only in this light that it can have a hidden meaning and a profoundly deep import. This meaning does not concern only the Polish nation, but it may be of international or supranational significance. (Primate Henryk Muszyński, April 19, 2010)

Spoken in a homily nine days after the disaster, these words by the then-Primate of Poland construe an emotionally appealing "Poland is Christ" metaphor, the strongest expression of the topos of Polish exceptionalism and moral superiority, perpetuated for years (Gomola 2019). The existence of this and the other religiously motivated conceptualizations in Polish public discourse detracts from the default neutrality of the meaning of the POLAND IS PERSON metaphor. Furthermore, it affects the related mappings, especially those involving the concept of BODY as the source domain. Specifically, the PERSON and BODY domains get charged with positive values, which the latter are projected on the NATION and STATE target domains. The effects are not so much conceptual, as pragmatic and strictly political: any encroachment on entities included in the NATION and STATE domains becomes morally contemptible. This whole mechanism goes a long way toward explaining, beyond the specific role of the BODY metaphor in texts such as (5), a broad presence of religious associations in L&J's discourse of governance in general.

Finally, the (C) NATION/STATE/GOVERNMENT IS TEAM metaphor develops a scenario that involves collective effort and continuing teamwork with a view to a final victory ("red and white team,[7] we will manage"). The coercive value of the scenario is that it activates, just like the A and B scenarios, a readily acceptable mental as well as behavioral pattern, based on embodied experience. In the case of the C scenario, the experience is derived from team sports, an element of the source domain of the POLITICS IS SPORTS metaphor. It involves, on the one hand, seeing collective effort as a necessary prerequisite for the final win and, on the other, seeing the win as a due reward for the effort. These mechanisms and relations within the sports domain are mapped, according to the POLITICS IS SPORTS metaphor, onto the political domain, establishing a self-evident, strong connection between political teamwork, the steadfastness of political purpose, and its likely victorious effects. Altogether, the scenario invoked by the NATION/STATE/GOVERNMENT IS TEAM metaphor is flexible with regard to who is considered as part of the "team." While the construal in (5) seems to include, principally, the L&J government and, by extension, the party, some broader interpretations involving supporters of L&J among Polish people are certainly possible.

As has been mentioned, the scenarios outlined in Kaczyński's narrative in (5) are closely followed in the later rhetoric, particularly in the years 2017–19:

(7) With "Family 500+" and other programs this government has taken a historic step to protect$_{A,B}$ economic safety of Polish families. Polish people deserve it; they deserve safety, equal rights and social justice. They deserve to feel masters of their own house$_B$. (Elżbieta Rafalska,[8] November 4, 2017)

(8) As long as we are proud of who we are and what we are fighting for$_A$, there is nothing beyond our reach. Most of the time after the transformation Poland was in the hands of post-communist officials having privileges of various sorts. They are afraid today that the times are changing, that the time has come when things will be as they are supposed to be. They are now trying to defend$_A$ their territory, but they are losing$_A$. (President Andrzej Duda, March 19, 2018)

(9) Each day since 2015, our team$_C$ has gone forward with a clear vision and a righteous mission— to make Poland a great common home$_B$ for all Poles. (Mateusz Morawiecki, September 26, 2018)

(10) But there was something else in those 8 years[9], which we must not forget. There was also a powerful collection of social pathologies that were created already in communism: criminal pathologies, pathologies tied to corruption, with the decay of the state apparatus, with its criminalization, with the situation in the special services. And a strong government had to fight$_A$ this. Mind you, this fight$_A$, this war$_A$, is not over. Poland is still, in many ways, a battlefield$_A$. (Joachim Brudziński,[10] May 5, 2019)

While texts (7)–(10) are quotes from different L&J politicians speaking on different occasions over the period of eighteen months, they convey, all together, a consistent narrative building on Kaczyński's message from the 2015 rally. In this narrative, the particular stances (less or more radical) and the respective scenarios are assigned to different speakers, according to their political status. Thus the hardest-hitting scenario, (A), is realized in an address by Minister of the Interior (10), and the scenario emerging from the HOME metaphor, (B), appears in a speech by Minister of Family, Labor and Social Policy (7). The (B) scenario is also enacted, interplaying with the TEAM metaphor, (C), in a brief comment from Prime Minister Mateusz Morawiecki in (9). The remaining example, (8), comes from a parliamentary address of Andrzej Duda, the president of Poland, whose election campaign was supported by the L&J party. It compares, quite apparently, with text (10) in terms of the scenario involved. However, the particular lexicalizations are somewhat less stirring and serving a more general focus, consistent with the political status of the speaker. As a result, text (8) is perhaps the closest in its rhetorical stance to Kaczyński's Tribunal speech. Among other analogies, it is worth noting that Kaczyński's notorious use of the word "pathology" to characterize the rule of the Civic Platform (and in fact the entire post-1989 period) is reflected in virtually the same kind of argument in (10). Incidentally, text (10) is also where the "in the past eight years" tale is invoked once again—four years after the government change. Finally, in text (9), the mention by Morawiecki of a "great common home" is commonly considered (e.g., Kłosińska and Rusinek 2019) an allusion to the slogan "make America great again," a phrase coined by Ronald Reagan but used most famously by Donald Trump in his 2016 presidential campaign.

3.3. Proximization

Throughout the 2015–19 term, L&J's discourse reveals ample use of proximization strategies. As has been explained in the first chapter, proximization is, technically, a conceptual operation that involves a forced construal of movement of entities within the symbolic *Them* camp in the direction of entities within the *Us* camp. The prospect of encroachment of the remote adversary generates a threat, which can be applied in the service of political coercion. Specifically, by projecting the outside adversary as encroaching, physically or ideologically, on the home camp, political speakers solicit legitimization of actions that they propose as preventive measures to stop the invasion.

As a conceptual as well as discourse pragmatic strategy, proximization inscribes into several schemata of conceptual metaphor. In particular, it draws on the capacity of metaphor to clearly demarcate and consolidate the opposing *Us* and *Them* camps. We have observed in the discussion of L&J's discourse in Section 3.2 that metaphoric construals of ideological opposition allow for a quick and efficient mobilization against the adversary, as well as legitimization of the suggested course of action. In addition, scenarios such as STATE IS BODY or STATE IS HOME provide an extra element of moral justification to actions aimed at protecting the *Us* camp against the hostile acts of the *Them* camp. The role of proximization in relation to these metaphoric construals is to present the virtual *Them*-toward-*Us* shift as maximally realistic and dynamic, and the resulting impact as maximally threatening.

The fact that proximization takes for granted the *Us* and *Them* underpinnings of political discourse makes it an ideal device to target political opponents. This function of proximization is corroborated in L&J's discourse, which makes use of different proximization strategies during the entire parliamentary term. In principle, in the years 2015–17 the L&J's stance on the parliamentary opposition (particularly Civic Platform) is expressed mostly in ideological terms, involving axiological proximization as the main strategy (though often assisted by other strategies). An example is this speech by Beata Szydło, the then–prime minister in the L&J government:

> **(11)** We have to redouble our efforts in the face of a threat that persists. We draw strength from the values that we hold dear: our families, our homes, our Christian faith. We must keep our eye fixed on the Poland we want to build—one that defeats our adversaries by promoting dignity, equal opportunity and justice. We must remain alert—lest we wake up, one day, in the old Poland. (Beata Szydło, parliamentary speech, October 21, 2017)

In Szydło's address, the framework for proximization is the opposition between values associated with the "home camp" represented by the current L&J government and the (presumably) antagonistic values associated with "the old Poland," denoting—presumably again—the post-transformation period and particularly the rule of the Civic Platform between 2007 and 2015. The need to make the two presumptions follows from the way in which the *Us* and *Them* camps are defined in the speech. While the *Us* camp is marked explicitly in terms of values such as "dignity," "opportunity," "justice," as well as religious and family values, the *Them* camp is defined implicitly by the implicature of contrary values indicating the adversary. The key lexical item triggering this implicature is the verb "defeat," which indirectly marks the *Them* values as conceptual opposites of "dignity," "justice," and so on. Emerging from this specific characterization is a generalized flashback vision of "the old Poland" as a country of injustice, social inequality, and ruthless, anti-family ideology.

Building on thus constructed conceptual opposition, the strategy of proximization involves construal of the antagonistic ideology as a "persisting threat" that is dormant yet able to (re-)appear, coming in the way of L&J's reforms to build a "new Poland." As Szydło's address in (11) is part of a parliamentary debate evaluating, from a two-year perspective, the results of multiple social programs passed by the L&J majority right after the elections, this threat can be read further—in material terms—as a potential encroachment on the continuation of these programs in case the CP opposition returns to power. The caliber and effects of the threat, and the emerging momentousness of the situation, are communicated via several mutually related construals involving cognitive, pragmalinguistic and lexical strategies and markers, such as indefinite descriptions, presupposition, and nominalizations.

The role of indefinite descriptions in threat generation consists in construing uncertainty of the future, conceptualized as a period that extends from the moment of speaking to an indefinite future point on the time axis. The threat element of such a conceptualization lies in the vagueness of the construed vision: it is impossible to determine the moment when the threat *could* materialize. The result is that anxiety levels rise, as the lack of clear outlines of the threat means that no specific countermeasures can be prescribed. In Szydło's speech, this mechanism is exploited in the closing sentence of the text. The threat is described as ominous yet unpredictable; it can happen "one day," but there is no remedy other than staying "alert." Of course, the latter judgment counts, in political terms, as a call to maintain support for the ruling party.

Elsewhere in (11), the threat is constructed and proximized in the use of forms and lexical items that are, individually and by themselves, triggers of conceptual conflations and the resulting underdefined and thus threatening visions. Such items are, notably, the noun "threat" itself, and the verb "persists," both occurring in the opening sentence. The former, as a nominalization, conflates the present and the future; it represents an objectified entity that exists at the present moment and presages an ominous future (Dunmire 2011). Doing so, it provides an ironically "precise" answer to the question when the threat can eventually "happen"—it can happen anytime. This answer might not, as we have noted, prescribe a clear course of action for the addressee, but it is nonetheless important from the speaker's legitimization perspective. Namely, it is a prerequisite for the speaker's flexibility of response: if the threat could materialize any moment, then any time is legitimate to act pre-emptively. The latter item, "persists," forces a similar conceptualization as regards the outlines of the threat and the moment of impact, adding, however, an important element of duration. This element helps extend the period of policy legitimization relative to the timeframe of the threat as defined arbitrarily by the speaker.

Finally, Szydło's text in (11) applies the mechanism of pragmatic presupposition to further enlarge the caliber of the threat. This mechanism involves, again, an ideologically loaded, ominous vision of reality that has changed entirely, negatively, and virtually overnight ("lest we wake up . . . in the old Poland"). The conjunction "lest" ["żeby nie"] has a crucial role to play: it makes the addressee take for granted the occurrence of the threatening change in case the current policy course is abandoned or ceases to attract popular support. The structuring of this message in terms of a presupposition makes the final inference (return to a past negative state) largely automatic (Dunmire 2011), facilitating acceptance of the message by the addressee.

From a theoretical standpoint, the analysis of Szydło's speech is a notable example of the interplay of axiological and temporal proximization. The axiological proximization in (11) can be considered in a way primary, as it draws on the most important conceptual property of the text, that is a conspicuous ideological difference and opposition between the *Us* and *Them* camps. In the process of cognitive shift enacted by discursive and linguistic means this opposition turns into a clash, which essentializes proximization— in this case axiological proximization—as a conceptual strategy of threat generation. However, the effects of thus generated threat, such as social mobilization and public acceptance of preventive means, require consideration in terms of temporal proximization. This is because all the coercive functions of the text involve, eventually, a symbolic shrinkage of the time axis, resulting in intensification of focus and centralization of the present timeframe. The pragmatic effects of such a centralization include strengthening the sense of momentousness of the current state of affairs and creating an extra impetus for taking preventive action.

In Cap (2013: 86), the centralization of the present timeframe (referred to as "now") in the process of temporal proximization has been shown in the form of a diagram depicting the particular timeframes and proximization shifts:

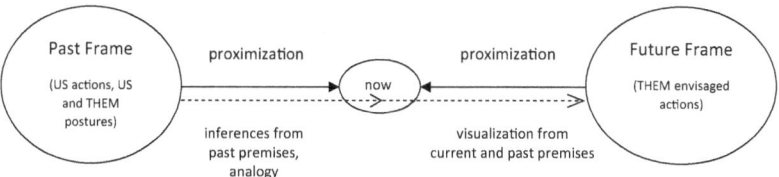

Figure 3.1 Centralizing *now* for momentousness: 2 temporal proximization shifts (adapted from Cap 2013: 86).

The general designations in Figure 3.1 can be applied to account for the conceptual relations evoked in (11).

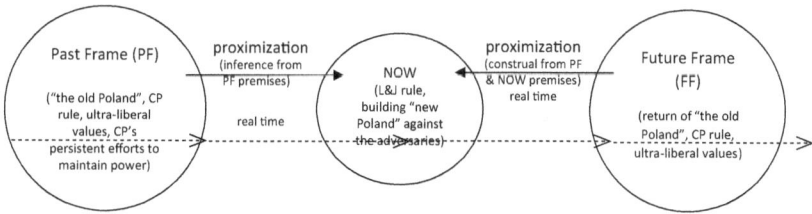

Figure 3.2 Temporal proximization in text (11).

Looking at Figure 3.2, we can speak of two kinds of conceptual relations established in text (11) in the process of proximization. Specifically, there are two complementary temporal channels via which text (11) generates its coercive powers. On the one hand, coercion is generated retrospectively, through a flashback vision of past reality. This vision includes, crucially, the image a potent adversary focused on holding political power. Simultaneously, there is a construal of a threateningly fragile character of the current political arrangement. In this arrangement, the adversary has been removed from power, but is likely to return, possibly in the near future (recall the "lest" phrase in the closing sentence of the text). Thus, the threat and the resulting coercive function of the text are construed in a twofold manner, within a pattern involving both retrospective and prospective conceptualizations. The result of the two construals taking place at the same time is a virtual shrinkage of the temporal axis. As the latter shrinks, the NOW frame and the actions it subsumes become critical to the future course of events.

The analysis of (11) shows that temporal projections provide axiological proximization with some extra coercive powers, derived from an extension of the *Us* and *Them* ideological conflict to cover a macro period of time, in which threats are constructed, reconstructed, and otherwise perpetuated by means of analogy, flashbacks, and temporal conflations. The same can be said of the interplay of temporal and spatial proximization, involving conceptualizations of the lasting presence of material threats. Spatiotemporal proximization is a core feature of texts representing a late stage of L&J's discourse in the 2015–19 term. During that stage, shortly before the 2019 elections, ideological argument gives way to hard-hitting, threatening visions involving spatiotemporal proximization strategies:

> **(12)** Let us remember. On this very day 6 years ago, the Civic Platform passed, in this house, an increase of the retirement age to 67. They'd been saying they would not do it but they did. We reversed it but they will do it again. That's part of their plan and we see it. It's getting clearer and clearer. So let us not get fooled again. Let us not vote for people who would make you work until death. (Jarosław Kaczyński, parliamentary speech, June 26, 2019)

Compared to Szydło's speech, the text in (12) redefines the threat in material (rather than ideological) terms. The vision of the CP party returning to power is construed as a physical invasion that can be "seen" and whose outlines get "clearer and clearer." The effects of the threat ("work until death") are construed in direct physical terms as well. The material character of such a conceptualization draws on the specificity of the issue discussed, which involves a physical process—of aging. Thus, the spatial proximization applied in (12) is at the same time a response to the existing context, and a contribution to an emerging context. The emerging context is essentially tangible, realistic, and ominous, revealing what appears a life threat. The vision of the threat is endorsed, as in (11), by a temporal projection. Specifically, a past moment is invoked ("on this very day 6 years ago"), serving to recall the betrayal of election promises by the CP party. This flashback is used to draw a precise temporal as well as spatial ("in this house") analogy, strengthening the credibility of the future vision. In general, text (11) conveys a strong coercive function, forcing a firm and clear-cut conceptual distinction between two futures: the promoted "privileged future" and a plainly threatening "alternative future" (Dunmire 2011).

Taken together, examples (11) and (12) demonstrate how L&J's discourse, particularly the rhetoric targeted at the parliamentary opposition, makes use of different proximization strategies to keep coercion levels high and thus secure legitimization of long-term leadership. At the beginning of the term, legitimization of L&J's rule rests on essentially ideological appeals and axiological proximization. There are two reasons for this. First, the ideological discourse that Kaczyński and his MPs engage in after the 2015 elections is directly related to and thematically consistent with L&J's discourse of the 2015 campaign. The common issues include security, family, tradition, equality, social programs, and, of course, harsh critique of the opposing priorities/values underlying the CP rule. Furthermore, with the elections just won, there is no need for a stronger instrument of coercion than ideological appeals, consolidating current support for the L&J party and the government. However, as the term goes on, new stimuli need to be created to reactivate the electorate before the next election campaign. Hence the switch to quick and effective fear appeals, involving construals of direct threats in the process of spatiotemporal proximization. Altogether, the interplay of different kinds of proximization in texts by L&J politicians defines the L&J discourse in general as a functional macro-discourse of legitimization (van Dijk 2007). As such, it is interesting to compare it, internationally, with other state-level discourses of a similar political status and range.

3.4. The European Populist Perspective: Hungary and Italy

Drawing analogies between L&J's discourse and other European party discourses is a complex multidimensional task, and our discussion in this book is necessarily limited to a few particularly interesting and analytically promising cases. These cases warrant further multidisciplinary research, involving tools and methods of not only (critical) discourse analysis but also communication studies, political science and, not least, comparative sociology. There are several planes on which comparisons can be made, from broadly sociopolitical, to political-discursive, to strictly linguistic. Apparently, the choice depends on the kind of analysis to which a comparison is supposed to contribute. The focus of this chapter has been on state-level communication and policy legitimization on the home front. Accordingly, we have looked at issues of direct and often urgent importance to home political audience such as security, employment, or retirement age. Communicating such issues, whether by L&J or any other ruling party, always involves a specific discursive style, as well as strategies which, on the one hand, increase public support for the party's "offer" and, on the other, lead to rejection of alternative offers put forward by the opposition. As has been demonstrated, Law & Justice has been highly successful in performing this kind of discourse, developing over the past few years into a model example of populist governance and communication. Consequently, in the discussion that follows we engage further with the concept of political populism, which we approach in terms of a rhetorical style. We use this concept to compare L&J's discourse with other party discourses in Europe, specifically Viktor Orban's and his FIDESZ party discourse in Hungary and the rhetoric of leaders of the Northern League and Five Star Movement in Italy.

Following Norris and Inglehart (2018), we take populist style as a combination of rhetorical features and strategies whereby political leaders pose as opponents and harsh critics of "corrupt and unpatriotic elites" and corrosive cosmopolitan liberalism together with its globalist policies, as well as defenders of "ordinary people," national identities and Christian traditions. Carrying the democratic mantle, they declare themselves the only genuine defenders of democracy, the latter understood as "people power" (62–5). They manipulate mass anxieties, fears, and hopes, and transform the politics of negotiation and compromise into the politics of direct confrontation and warfare. According to Norris and Inglehart (2018), the distinctive characteristics of populist style include:

- anti-elite, anti-establishment rhetoric and orientation. Populists portray the established elites as corrupt, self-interested, arrogant, exploitative and often treacherous;

- self-representation as sole legitimate "servants of the people." Populists claim to be the sole democrats and the sole authentic representatives of "ordinary people." All others are portrayed as illegitimate;

- use of emotionally loaded language. Populists specialize in vitriolic attacks on their opponents—seen as enemies, rather than rivals. They appeal to emotions, rather than reason, and stir these emotions—especially fear, resentment and hope—skillfully using a broad range of mass media, especially social media;

- the promise of quick and direct solutions to the key problems and challenges that the country faces. Populists (ab)use discourse to promise to clean up politics ("drain the swamp"[11]); bring real justice; vindicate "the people's will," defend national sovereignty and restore dignity to "the people." (Norris and Inglehart 2018: 66)

These features define the rhetorical dimension of what Norris and Inglehart (2018) call "contemporary authoritarian populism" (: 65). The latter can be understood as a cultural backlash against long-term ongoing social change. On this view, parties such as Law & Justice or FIDESZ express a general protest against the checks and balances system introduced to prevent "the people's direct rule." They seek to undermine the universality of democracy and to erode liberal-democratic norms, replacing them with new counter-norms that emphasize state security and traditional values.

Norris and Inglehart's seminal research is largely in agreement with what is perhaps the most recent study in populist discourse to date, that is, Schneider and Eitelmann's analysis of Donald Trump's rhetoric (2020). Drawing on discourse of Trump's 2016–20 presidency, Schneider and Eitelmann invite us to place special emphasis on the following features of populist style:

- a dualistic worldview consisting of the positively connoted people and the negatively connoted elite;

- presenting political actions as being in the common interest of "the people"; thus, disregarding minority interests.

The first characteristic may look obvious but, according to Schneider and Eitelmann (2020), discourses such as Trump's show that the core bipolar notions of "people" and "elite" are essentially constructed categories, whose boundaries may shift and are unlikely to be spelled out. Thus, the boundaries remain fuzzy and vague descriptors are used. In Trump's discourse, this means ample use of impersonal stance devices, which express speaker's stance without assuming responsibility for that stance. The devices in question are, for example, adverbs such as "actually," "obviously," and "certainly" (all highly common in Donald Trump's speeches), which make reference to information that is apparently "actual," "obvious," and "certain," yet without providing evidentiality (Schneider and Eitelmann 2020: 33).

The other point is an equally worthwhile addition, highlighting the fact that since in a Manichean, dualistic worldview the "bad" is represented by a minority elite, the "good" can possibly be a minority; it must not represent interests other than shared by the masses. Indeed, this is something to bear in mind, not only in the discussion herein but mainly as we turn to the "worst sort" narrative in the next chapter.

3.4.1. Orban's Revolutionary Rhetoric

Analogies between L&J's discourse and FIDESZ's leadership discourse (meaning, essentially, PM Viktor Orban's rhetoric) in Hungary must be considered in a broader political and historical context. This context subsumes, first of all, an idea of "a special Polish-Hungarian friendship" (Agh 2016), which has developed over many years of shared history, from Stefan Batory, a Hungarian-born king of Poland in the sixteenth century, to Polish people's solidarity with the anti-communist Hungarian Revolution of 1956. Indeed, a saying in both languages speaks of "a Pole and a Hungarian, two blood brothers." A resolution establishing a day of Polish-Hungarian friendship, passed by the Polish parliament in 2007, draws on how the two nations have pushed back multiple "threats from east and west."

We must also note that the Polish-Hungarian relationship has gained in significance after Law & Justice came to power in 2015. The L&J government and the FIDESZ government converge on many points, for instance their vision of Europe. Here, neither wants to leave the EU; instead, they want to reform it from within. Both favor a Europe of nation-states based upon voluntary cooperation and thus have opposed the EU's forced relocation of refugees from the Middle East, presenting it as an interference in internal affairs. In April 2018, Jarosław Kaczyński and Mateusz Morawiecki paid a visit to Budapest to support FIDESZ in the Hungarian parliamentary elections. Celebrating his party's third consecutive victory, Viktor Orban thanked the Polish delegation profusely, emphasizing the mutual appreciation between the governments in Warsaw and Budapest. Speaking in front of the Hungarian Parliament, he invited Kaczyński and Morawiecki onto the stage, saying, "There is an old saying in Hungary that if you trust somebody, like we trust each other, 'you can steal horses together.'" In response, Kaczyński declared, "I am convinced that next year we will have Budapest in Warsaw," thus indicating his hopes to emulate FIDESZ's continuing electoral success (Hungary Today, April 15, 2018).

That said, it is hardly surprising to see rhetorical similarities between the two parties, though naturally there are some distinctive characteristics on each side. In their study of Hungarian populist discourse, Szilagyi and Bozoki (2015) describe Viktor Orban's style as a so-called "revolutionary rhetoric," practiced consistently since FIDESZ's victory in 2010 parliamentary elections. The origins of this rhetoric go back even further, to Orban's memorable speech given on June 16, 1989. The speech took place at the reburial ceremony of the executed Prime Minister of the 1956 anti-Soviet Hungarian Revolution, Imre Nagy, and was heard by an audience of 250,000 at the Heroes' Square in Budapest, while millions of Hungarians followed it live on television. In his address, Orban, who was then a newcomer to politics and had formed the FIDESZ party only a year before, articulated simultaneously emotional and radical demands for the immediate withdrawal of Soviet troops from Hungary and the announcement of free parliamentary elections. The address met with a huge success, becoming one of the key pro-democracy speeches in Hungarian history, and playing a decisive role in FIDESZ's win in the subsequent elections. As such, it became a lasting symbol of Victor Orban's rhetoric involving three interrelated elements: the address "on behalf of" the people, the announcement of a groundbreaking change, and the appeal to national unity in a critical historical moment. As argued by Szilagyi and Bozoki (2015), the presence of these three elements was the first property that earned Orban's rhetoric its "revolutionary" label.

Studying the evolution of Viktor Orban's discourse in later years and especially after the 2010 elections, Szilagyi and Bozoki (2015) point to some further features that can be named as "revolutionary," despite the absence of the original, 1989 rhetorical setting. All of these features count simultaneously among the central characteristics of populist style as defined by Norris and Inglehart (2018) and, as will be evident, all are shared by Kaczyński and other L&J politicians in Poland. Notably, Orban's speeches are nearly always part of large public events, following a strict dramaturgy. This involves performances by popular artists and speeches by other FIDESZ party officials, and, finally, Orban's address, to which party supporters react with open enthusiasm: waving national flags, holding support banners, and chanting the Prime Minister's first name. Agh (2016) observes that such rallies are more than simply "political theater," they offer an "experience of collectivity" (: 37). He notes that between 2010 and 2015, Orban delivered several major speeches a year on the streets and in the arenas of Budapest, and these were always attended by large crowds. Consequently, the occasions were reported as "grand," "momentous," and "historic" by the Hungarian media, even though they were not such in the real sense of the term. Unlike Orban's 1989 address, they did not take place in the context of important historical events and did not carry any special news or messages that should electrify public attention. However, the sheer size and character of these public occasions has been, and still is, a major factor in Orban's construction of himself as a leader that speaks and acts on behalf of the people.

At the linguistic level, Orban's discourse and his enactment of leadership are equally well thought out, involving an ample presence of forms, phrases, and individual words invoking national unity and pride. At the same time, the sense of national unity is set against challenges of the current moment, which, in Orban's discourse, is nearly always "historic" and bringing a "groundbreaking change" (Szilagyi and Bozoki 2015). The key linguistic items responsible for these construals are lexical markers of plurality, especially first-person plural pronouns, and common nouns. Accordingly, the pronominal choices in Viktor Orban's speeches, both after and before 2010, are predominantly the "we," "us," and "our" deictic choices ("If *we* believe in our strength. . ." / "If *we* are determined enough. . ." / "*Our* goals remain the same [as in 1989]") (Viktor Orban, May 4, 2014). They are usually accompanied by common noun keywords such as "Hungarians," "people," as well as nouns stressing the apparent homogeneity of different social subgroups, such as "pensioners," "mothers," or "youth." Altogether, the function of the aforementioned markers is not only to enact unity but also to imply that the audience of speeches which include these ploys is virtually equivalent to the whole Hungarian nation. This underlying exclusionary message is salient in two famous comments made by Viktor Orban right before the announcement of the results of exit polls in the 2014 parliamentary elections ("of course we will win, the nation cannot be in opposition," and "the country expects our common cause to win") (Viktor Orban, April 6, 2014).

Finally, Orban enacts his revolutionary stance through the frequent use of the word "revolution" itself, which he applies in various contexts on different occasions but typically during election campaigns. In fact, "revolution" occurs repeatedly in three consecutive election discourses, during the 2010, 2014, and 2018 parliamentary campaigns:

> **(13)** There were several such moments in Hungarian history. In the middle of the twentieth century the revolution in 1948 or the revolution in 1956 were like this, and for us the regime change in 1990 was also like this. And today, we Hungarians have arrived again at such a day. We arrive at a new one, among the rare great days of history, Hungarian history. (Viktor Orban, April 11, 2010)
>
> **(14)** Today a revolution took place at the polls. (Viktor Orban, April 6, 2014)
>
> **(15)** Today in Hungary, in these elections, we learned a historical lesson, that is the lesson of the past 28 years, that is the lesson of the regime change, and that is as follows: it is impossible to change a regime, a regime can be only brought down and overthrown by a revolution, overthrown and replaced by a new one. (Viktor Orban, April 8, 2018)

Examples (13–15) represent Orban's comments made on the 2010, 2014, and 2018 election nights. In all these comments, "revolution" serves to express the groundbreaking character of FIDESZ's projected victory. Interestingly, "revolution" is used to denote not only the first victory (in 2010) but also the subsequent wins, constituting not an assumption but a renewal of power. Furthermore, in all the three cases, Orban's "revolution" appears to be taking place in a peaceful political context, defined by the existence of democratic institutions and legal procedures. This shows that, in Orban's rhetoric, the concept of revolution is construed discursively in an essentially symbolic way, as a trigger of popular mobilization against the current political or social challenge. Such a strategy bears much resemblance, in its coercive function, to the conceptual centralization of the "now" timeframe that we have observed in L&J's discourse. In both cases, the aim is a quick, broad, and unconditional legitimization of policies. It is accomplished through the forced conceptualization of people's future as directly dependent on the suggested common way to meet the challenge.

In regard to its stance on the political opposition in Hungary, Orban's rhetoric is apparently somewhat less radical than that of L&J. While it does include references to "corrupt elites" and "oligarchs," it does not immediately associate the latter with the parliamentary opposition, as is clearly the case with Kaczyński's discourse. The *Us*-and-*Them* divide is not quite as explicit either, though increasingly salient especially since FIDESZ's second consecutive win in 2014 (Szilagyi and Bozoki 2015). Instead, the *Us* camp is construed as highly forceful and sociopolitically dominant, and the *Them* camp is discursively marginalized. As a result, threat levels are markedly lower than in L&J's discourse. In Orban's rhetoric, policy legitimization draws not so much on the necessity of response created by the emergence of a specific threat, but rather on the imperative imposed by the "will of the people," grounded in the sense of loyalty to the ideals of the 1990 democratic transition. This does not detract from the coercive power of such an imperative; as has been noted, the construal of momentousness of the "now" frame is an equally distinctive feature of both Orban's and L&J's discourse. Still, Orban's rhetorical style seems, as a whole, somewhat less definable in terms of individual strategies of coercion, such as metaphoric scenarios or proximization. In regard to the latter, while discourse space itself is well defined by deictic choices such as pronominals, there are few pragmalinguistic forms that can carry the essential, fear-inducing proximization shifts. Thus, the most fruitful plane on which to compare Orban's rhetoric and L&J's discourse remains its populist design and overtone. Here, numerous analogies arise with respect to virtually all the characteristics (Norris and Inglehart 2018), particularly in the area of conceptual self-representation and discursive performance of leadership. Indeed, the modern leadership discourse in Poland and Hungary is a discourse whereby both governments undertake to speak on behalf of the people and enact the popular will. Simultaneously, however, it is a discourse of leadership that gives way, in the words of Pakulski (2018: 21), to opportunistic "fellowship," under which liberal democracy transforms into "a public-opinion driven plebiscitarian leader democracy."

3.4.2. The (Northern) League and the Five Star Movement

In this final part of the chapter, we move from Hungary to Italy, to discuss the discourse of two leading political parties commonly considered as populist (Mazzoleni and Bracciale 2018): the League (known as the Northern League until 2018) and the Five Star Movement (henceforth M5S: Movimento Cinque Stelle). This time our focus is not so much on the strictly linguistic, lexico-grammatical intricacies of the discourse as such, but rather on the way in which it is communicated. Specifically, it is upon how the mode of communication—the online mode—interacts with and eventually strengthens the political message conveyed. Indeed, both M5S and the League are credited for a distinctive ability to use online channels to set up a close bond of relationship with their supporters (Bracciale and Martella 2017). While on the populist rhetorical plane their discourse does not really include any extra element compared to, for instance, L&J's or FIDESZ's discourse, many argue that it is precisely that closeness and communicative appeal that explain M5S and the League's political success (Bobba 2018; Mazzoleni and Bracciale 2018).

The greatest symbol of this success have been, without doubt, the results of the 2018 parliamentary elections in Italy. The center-right coalition, whose main party was the League led by Matteo Salvini, emerged with a plurality of seats in the Chamber of Deputies and in the Senate, while the Five Star Movement led by Luigi Di Maio took, altogether, the largest number of votes (32%). Since during the elections no political group or party won an outright majority, the subsequent government formation involved long party negotiations, but eventually a coalition was established between M5S and the League. As a result, Salvini and Di Maio became Deputy Prime Ministers in a government led by the independent Giuseppe Conte as Prime Minister. The coalition ended with Conte's resignation in August 2019 after the League pulled its support of the government. Subsequently, a new coalition agreement was signed by M5S and the center-left Democratic Party.

In their comprehensive analysis of the 2018 campaign, Mazzoleni and Bracciale (2018) attribute the unprecedented success of M5S and the League to their ability to convince voters to appreciate online communication, particularly Facebook-based communication, as "a new and effective form of direct democracy, putting the power back in the hands of the people" (2018: 2). They note that the online communication environment frequently allows for the circumvention of traditional opinion leaders and facilitates what is called the "one-step flow of communication." At the same time the horizontality and ubiquitousness of platforms such as FB allow a vast circulation of populist content with high potential impact. These features of online communication have been amply exploited by M5S and the League's leaders. But most of all, the use of online platforms of communication is crucial in instilling among people "the idea of political cooperation and co-construction of future vision proposed by the political leader" (Mazzoleni and Bracciale 2018: 3). The effect is the emergence of a sense of collective responsibility, and, over time, a rise of mutual confidence. In Mazzoleni and Bracciale's (2018) view, it is this last advantage of online communication that is ultimately decisive for the leader's final success. It is also the feature that has been exploited most efficiently by both parties' politicians.

Further, Mazzoleni and Bracciale (2018) observe that the themes constituting the core content of the campaigns of M5S and the League have been carefully shaped to meet the contextual conditions of the social media environment, especially the condition of vast public participation. Exploring Facebook timelines of Matteo Salvini and Luigi Di Maio in the last months before the elections, they conclude that both leaders have based their campaign rhetoric almost completely upon a complex and multidimensional "appeal to the people," thus acknowledging popular will as the only legitimate source of political change. Indeed, looking at texts analyzed by Mazzoleni and Bracciale (2018), one can notice that the kind of popular call by Salvini and Di Maio differs in many ways from similar appeals in the rhetoric of other populist leaders relying predominantly on traditional media, like Orban or Kaczyński. The difference lies in the conceptual underpinnings as well as implications of the call, specifically the complex way in which the concept of "the people" is employed and verbalized to maximize the unity of the electorate. Notwithstanding some minor individual differences between the two rhetorical styles, both Salvini and Di Maio approach "the people" in fixed relation to the general concept of sovereignty. On this view, "the people" is the ultimate democratic sovereign or the "ruler," often betrayed by the elites. Thus, the people's will should be a fundamental principle for all political actors, who become advocates of the people's rights. In the following post Di Maio expresses his awareness of this principle:

> **(16)** Above all, I feel the suffering of Italians who feel unsafe in their homes, harassed by taxes, disillusioned with politics and anti-politics. And I feel a great responsibility. More and more Italians are asking me, right here on FB, to radically change things that are wrong in our country. To put an end to fiscal oppression, bureaucratic oppression and judicial oppression. The people are asking and the people are always right. (Luigi Di Maio on Facebook, February 2, 2018)

Second, Salvini and Di Maio position "the people" in the context of long-standing and oppressive social divisions. They refer to the people as "underprivileged citizens who differ from the elites mainly with respect to their economic situation, formal education and access to power" (Mazzoleni and Bracciale 2018: 4). Accordingly, "the people" are depicted as a deprived socioeconomic class or subset of the population disregarded by consecutive governments and political elites. This underprivileged status gives "the people" a moral right to demand participation in the country's leadership:

> **(17)** Not only will we redo the 200€ but we will raise the bonus to 400 because this measure serves to restore purchasing power to the elderly after all these years. The members of parliament don't give a toss about all this because they get high pensions at the age of 65 for having worked for just four and a half years. It is the right of the people, of all hard-working citizens, to see this injustice gone. It is our responsibility to make it gone. (Matteo Salvini on Facebook, January 16, 2018)

Finally, the concept of "the people" is construed in terms of a national community or ethnic group. Both Salvini and Di Maio put emphasis on belonging to the native population as the main criterion to discriminate who is part or not part of the nation:

> **(18)** The Democratic Party is insisting by all means on enactment of the new Ius Soli law. It is a wrong law that Italians do not want. We want it to be possible for those who feel truly Italian to become Italian, not those who have only gone through a few bureaucratic steps. Perhaps the Democratic Party hopes to create a pool of new voters in this way. There is even talk of 800,000 people. If so I must say that it is a short-sighted and also cynical calculation on the skin of the people. (Luigi di Maio on Facebook, February 10, 2018)

In (18), Di Maio's argument proceeds in a subtle inferential pattern involving textual cohesion, as well as discursive and logical coherence. First, anaphoric reference is used ("Italians"—"We") to conflate two conceptual domains: the identity domain and the domain of political representation. Di Maio suggests that the only representation of Italians that is truly faithful to Italian identity is that by the M5S party. All alternatives, implies his argument, are not "Italian enough." Di Maio's conceptualization of the main political opponent, the Democratic Party, as a representative of "new voters" has a strong exclusionary value: it distances the Democratic Party from the "true Italians." As a result, the only representative of "the people" remains M5S. In the absence of political alternatives, it is perceived as not just a party but in fact the political embodiment of the nation.

Altogether, examples such as (18) show that the "appeal to the people" in the discourse of M5S and the League performs a complex rhetorical function, which includes, also, assertion of the presence of a strong and potentially threatening political adversary. While Salvini and Di Maio make a moderate use of direct fear appeals (except in their anti-immigration rhetoric; see Mazzoleni and Bracciale 2018), their discourse can still be described as essentially coercive, forcing construals of opposing ideological representations to secure mobilization of the home camp. These construals are, however, different in comparison with the Polish and Hungarian discourses, in that they involve resources other than the standard conceptual schemas of threat construction, such as proximization. Unlike L&J's discourse and Orban's rhetoric, the discourse of M5S and the League focuses, conceptually, on the *Us* party, taking the sense of security of the *Us* entities in the home camp as the main source of coercion. As a result, the concept of the central *Us* entity, "the people," is also far more complex and elaborate than the respective concepts in the Polish and Hungarian discourses. Finally, the notion of social solidarity that underlies the discourse of both Italian parties reveals the crucial feature of rhetorical velocity, which ensures further circulation and coercion effects. As has been discussed, the velocity feature makes it possible for positive or reassuring messages to be recomposed and subsequently redistributed by their original recipients. In effect, the target audience broadens, as the recipients are usually happy to share the positive, beneficial, or simply "good-sounding" message further.

4

The "Worst Sort of Poles" Narrative

On December 6, 2015, about 100,000 people took to the streets of Warsaw, protesting against a raft of changes being introduced by Law & Justice to all levels of the Polish judicial system. Accusing the L&J government of undermining the rule of law and flouting the Constitution, protesters called on EU organizations, particularly the European Commission and the Venice Commission,[1] to review the new laws. A few days later, in his interview for *Gazeta Polska*, the L&J leader Jarosław Kaczyński made a memorable response to these calls:

> (1) This is a return to the methods of 2005-2007.[2] This habit of denouncing Poland to foreigners. In Poland there is a fatal tradition of national treason. And this is precisely tied to that. It is sort of in the genes of some people, the worst sort of Poles. And that worst sort is precisely now extraordinarily active, because they feel threatened. Just consider that WWII, then communism, then the transformation were carried out in the way they were carried out: precisely this type of person dominated, was given every chance. They are afraid today that the times are changing, that the time is coming when things will be as they are supposed to be, and another type of person—that means, those having loftier, patriotic motivations—will be placed in the lead, and that will apply to every aspect of social life, including economic life. (Jarosław Kaczyński, December 11, 2015)

From the present perspective, these words by Kaczyński can be taken as the beginning of a distinctive rhetorical pattern, making a key contribution to L&J's home-front discourse over the entire 2015–19 term. We refer to this pattern as the "worst sort of Poles" narrative—a macro-temporal conceptual and discursive strategy of instilling social divisions and deliberately provoking social conflicts and crises in the country, in order to create conditions for the enactment of strong leadership and effective policy legitimization.

In this chapter, we explore the "worst sort of Poles" narrative as applying to different social groups construed by Law & Justice as more or less open opponents to the party's "reformatory" policies introduced after the 2015 elections. Unlike in the previous chapter, where our focus was on formal parliamentary opposition, we now concentrate on a multitude of groups of the so-called ordinary Poles that have come, since 2015, into some kind of political (or sometimes legal) conflict with the ruling party, and thus have experienced persecution by state institutions or, most typically, virulent propaganda attacks from the state-controlled media. Included in these groups (or rather one common out-group) are basically all those whose ideologies clash, according to L&J, with the Polish national values (as defined by the ruling party). This makes the "worst sort" a truly heterogeneous community: from legal activists and defenders of the constitutional order, to feminist groups, to LGBT groups and supporters of minority rights, to environmentalists urging a decrease in coal production (a "national treasure" of Poland, in L&J's discourse) to curb pollution, among others. In L&J's view, the activity of most of these groups, such as the LGBT community in Poland, is heavily inspired by foreign ideologies and thus should be considered anti-Polish. The latter conclusion is used in turn as a premise for a logical shortcut to call the followers "national traitors," as Kaczyński did in his press interview.

The present chapter shows how the aforementioned argument, underlying the "worst sort of Poles" narrative, is enacted in the service of conceptual othering through the use of specific cognitive and pragmalinguistic strategies, such as deictic distancing, metaphorization, and proximization (axiological and temporal). It demonstrates the ways in which these strategies and the narrative as a whole connect with the new historical narration, historical revisionism, and the general trend of "rewriting history" characterizing the rule of Law & Justice from day one after the elections. It is shown, for instance, how L&J's discourse exploits difficult and often tragic events in Polish history (such as the partitions of Poland in the eighteenth century, events during the Second World War, and, most recently, the Smolensk air disaster in 2010), invoking their memories instrumentally to establish "analogies" to legitimize the party's anti-liberal stance and the growing control of the state over the social, political, and economic domains of the public space. Finally, it is observed that the "worst sort" narrative, albeit controversial (and certainly cynical from a moral perspective), reveals a number of thematic as well as conceptual connections to other European discourses, especially in Balkan countries such as Romania and Bulgaria.

4.1. Good Poles and Bad Poles

In its conceptual design, the "worst sort of Poles" narrative relies on a dichotomous representation of Polish people in terms of two social groups revealing major ideological differences with regard to a number of consequential issues of morality, truth, national heritage, and collective memory. We shall refer to these groups as a "liberal camp" and a "solidarity camp." The "liberal vs. solidarity" ideological distinction counts among the most popular conceptual structures in L&J's discourse, particularly in the discourse of its leader Jarosław Kaczyński. It has been invoked tens of times in his speeches, comments, and interviews during the 2015–19 term (Wylęgalski 2019). For this reason, the following argument quotes mainly from Kaczyński, rather than any other L&J politician.

On Kaczyński's view, the liberal camp is defined in political-economic terms of a broad and orthodox commitment to free market capitalism and ultra-liberal, socially ruthless rule. It possesses some more specific features, too, but these have been discussed in the previous chapter and we do not readdress them here. Crucially, members of the liberal camp recognize rule of law as the central and virtually the only source of legitimacy of the state. This is, however, not the rule of law in Locke's or Dicey's noble sense of tyranny prevention (cf. Erman 2018). According to Kaczyński, the concept of "law" has not only positive but also negative, aspects and connotations: law is negotiable and thus always the result of a political compromise, which often ignores the moral rights and needs of the people to whom the law applies and in whose interest it should be designed. Thus, above the law there is always "will of the people," a supreme moral imperative and the only true mandate to act and govern in the name and interest of the nation. This mandate is granted, according to Kaczyński, to those who hold a political majority as they are embodiment of the will of the social majority that elected them.

Interestingly, the concept of the "will of the people" as superior to "law" was initially invoked not by Jarosław Kaczyński himself, but by Kornel Morawiecki, a Law & Justice MP and father of Prime Minister Mateusz Morawiecki.[3] However, in his 2015–19 speeches and comments, Kaczyński makes ample references to the apparent axiological conflict between the two imperatives. His classic example is the Constitution of Poland, whose passing (in April 1997) he considers a much faulty result of a purely political compromise under the government of the Social Democracy of the Republic of Poland (SdRP). SdRP was created in 1991 by people associated with the former communist party (the Polish United Workers' Party), and thus Kaczyński has long been a harsh critic of the Constitution, calling it "another [after the Round Table agreement] deal with the communists."[4]

How does the concept of the "worst sort" and the narrative emerge from all this? The answer is as quick as it is frightening. The "good Poles" are simply all those who believe in the superiority of the will of a popular majority over a code of law. The "bad Poles" are those who do not share such a belief, thus contesting, in Kaczyński's view, not only the legitimacy of the state but also the collective identity and morality of its people. The "worst sort" are finally all those who, in addition, make their "unpatriotic" ideologies public and/or communicate them abroad. In his interview for *Gazeta Polska* (cf. (1) earlier) Kaczyński considers such practices the main strategy of the liberal opposition, which he sums up by the phrase "ulica i zagranica" (*lit.* "the street and foreign countries"). The phrase, very popular over the entire 2015–19 period and a core element of the "worst sort" narrative, is supposed to reveal what Kaczyński thinks are the real aspirations of the opposition: sowing unrest in the country and informing on the Polish government to the EU.

The above characterization of the "worst sort" makes the term apply, first of all, to all those who have found themselves, under the L&J government, as more or less open/active defenders of the country's constitutional order against policies that violate the rule of law under the "will/good of the people" banner.[5] This makes not only lawyers or legal activists but in fact many ordinary people, such as the 100,000 street protesters in Warsaw, a direct target of the narrative. On every occasion throughout 2015–19, Kaczyński asserts that by democratically assuming state power, Law & Justice is entitled to make far-reaching changes in the public domain. As state constitutes a supreme moral value reflecting a dominant national morality based upon tradition, collective identity, and preservation of collective memory, it also assumes a regulatory function in order to recognize these values and implement them through policies it produces. Kaczyński sets out such a vision in the speech given during Independence Day celebrations in 2016:

> **(2)** The white-red flag is a symbol of our state, a symbol stipulated in the constitution. Symbols are meant to build unity, to create unity. But simultaneously symbols are meant to remind, to make aware that there is a direct relationship between public sphere/state sphere, and sphere of values. A fundamental truth is at stake. Not only is the state an organization covering certain territory; the state should constitute a moral quality. We have talked about it for over 20 years. I wish to repeat it now once again. This moral quality, to put it somehow differently, means a legitimacy of the state. (Jarosław Kaczyński, November 11, 2016)

In this fragment, Kaczyński puts an emphasis on moral quality of the state, but also refers indirectly to the role of collective memory when he invokes national symbols as its principal carriers. Since symbols are viewed as unifying all citizens, they stand for a uniform set of values represented by the state and its institutions that authorize them. Crucially, as authority of the state reaches beyond regulatory functions and assumes a moral position, it also sanctions certain modes of behavior or attitudes and bans others. As long as the stance of the state externalized in normative acts matches with morality of the people, it can be called legitimate. We can see that although Kaczyński departs from the concept of symbol as a semiotic embodiment of values, the role of national symbols is not the focal point of his argument. The crux of the argument involves the relationship between the state, political legitimacy, and morality, as reflected in L&J's conception of politics over years of the party's existence. Developing the theme of morality in a later part of the speech, Kaczyński proposes a threefold concept of state legitimacy:

> **(3)** We can talk about two types of legitimacy, except the one which is very important to democracy and which by no means I intend to ignore, namely formal legitimacy, i.e. the legitimacy which stems from constitutional regulations, law-making regulations, from all that pertains to democracy and which we do not want to dispute. <u>But there are legitimacies which are deeper, so to say.</u>[6] We can talk about two such legitimacies. The first is of historical—moral character. It involves history, tradition, language, culture codes, common understanding and understanding of meaning. This legitimacy is extremely important as it is linked to social awareness; but in the case of Poland, Polish tradition, it pertains to some clearly stated

postulates. These postulates are—freedom, equality and justice. The second type of legitimacy, which may be called a pragmatic one, concerns all these things which the state is supposed to provide. In other words, it means everything the state does in order to satisfy the needs of citizens and of the community. These two legitimacies are non-negotiable. Whoever tries to oppose them, often on the grounds of some legal tricks, opposes the nation in its entirety. (Jarosław Kaczyński, November 11, 2016)

This text constitutes the clou of Kaczyński's argument, defining L&J's stance on the most critical issues of governance and as such providing a firm framework to distinguish, in ideological and moral terms, between the party's supporters, the opponents, and those of the "worst sort" who contest the legality of L&J's rule. Apart from democratic mandate based on procedural principles, Kaczyński lists two other legitimacies: historical—moral and pragmatic as indispensable for the modern state. In the first case, legitimacy is externalized through manifestations of freedom and equality in expressing cultural and national affiliation. This means that nursing public awareness of national historical legacy and culture becomes a moral imperative of the state. Therefore, history becomes a subject of moral judgment under state tutelage and constitutes a determinant of current condition of public awareness based on the historical and moral continuity carried by various state-sanctioned manifestations of memory in the public space. Tradition, on the other hand, provides a set of indisputable values that serve as a benchmark for such historical-moral judgments. The second of the two legitimacies which Kaczyński describes as "deeper" is externalized in economic and personal security domains. Pragmatic legitimacy, as he calls it, pertains to the role of the state as a producer and supplier of economic goods that ensure existential security of its citizens. The conclusion from this entire exposé is as follows. As long as the state derives its policies from what it declares to be historical, ideological, and moral national heritage and as long as it provides economically for the people, the "legality" of these policies becomes secondary. Those who do not understand it or, even worse, oppose it—the "worst sort"—deserve moral exclusion as they compromise the central values of the nation and the state.

Next to the concept of state legitimacy are in Kaczyński's discourse the domains of national memory and truth, which he exploits to draw further ideological and moral distinctions. Notably, the solidarity camp—the "good Poles"—are conceptualized as staunch defenders of national memory, especially the memory of tragic events such as the Smolensk crash. In contrast, those who do not engage in or at least support the state-organized commemorations of such events are construed as morally inferior, lacking personal honesty and integrity. This is because, according to Kaczyński, by not supporting the commemorations they hinder clearing up any non-transparent issues surrounding the events. This in turn makes them—the "worst sort of Poles"—political accomplices of those who might have an interest in *not* clearing such issues and thus covering up what might be the "real causes." Kaczyński's speech from the April 10, 2016, rally commemorating the Smolensk crash illustrates this reasoning very well:

> (4) They [the Civic Platform government] wanted to kill our memory. They wanted to kill it, because they feared it. Because someone is responsible for this tragedy, at least morally, no matter what were the causes of it. And this responsibility lies with the previous government. And they did everything, breaking the rules in every possible manner, to make this memory perish. As did their supporters and the whole Polish establishment, who claim to have right to control both Poland and Polish memory. But their actions were unsuccessful, unsuccessful from the beginning. This memory lasted already on the first days. The first memorials appeared, commemorations took place, independent press and independent media covered this topic. (Jarosław Kaczyński, April 10, 2016)

On Kaczyński's view, memory, or rather the act of commemoration as its manifestation, amounts to a moral imperative that is naturally superior over the establishment of facts ("someone is responsible . . . no matter what were the causes"). Consequently, construal of memory, especially collective memory, becomes the central criterion and determiner of objective truth. In (4) Kaczyński seeks to monopolize a uniform ("our") understanding of memory by claiming the right to represent as well as interpret moral standards of collectivity while at the same time rejecting any argumentations that do not encompass the moral dimension of memory. This allows him to depict those who do not support the state in the way it organizes Smolensk commemorations as deeply immoral, unpatriotic, evil people whose aim is to "kill our [i.e. national] memory," in order to prevent the "good Poles" from accessing "public truth":

> (5) This truth [about the Smolensk catastrophe] can be defined as public truth, state truth, truth in textbooks, truth in books, truth in media, in the generally available media, truth in the awareness of Poles, as <u>millions of</u>

Poles, the righteous ones, do not know what happened, do not understand it all. We must explain it to them, because the previous government wouldn't. Because their supporters and their media wouldn't.[7] We must use the possibilities we have today in order to make Poles realize and understand it. Today, as the research shows, almost 25% of young people cannot answer the question—Who is responsible for the Katyń massacre? Today, we cannot let it happen in the case of Smolensk. (Jarosław Kaczyński, April 10, 2016)

Apart from enacting moral, ideological as well as political distinctions, Kaczyński performs in (5) an important legitimization strategy that involves using flashbacks of past events to endorse current visions and political judgments. In this particular case, he draws an analogy between the Smolensk crash and the massacre of Polish military officers carried out by the Soviet secret police during the Second World War.[8] The core elements of the analogy are the victims (military elite then vs. state-political elite now), mutually close locations, and, crucially, long-term controversies over the "real responsibility" for both events. While the first two elements (the victims and the locations) are quite obviously valid, the third element (the responsibility) detracts from the correctness of the analogy as a whole. While the responsibility of the Soviet Union for the Katyń massacre has been thoroughly studied, documented, and confirmed, in the light of the current evidence no such responsibility can be attributed to Russia for the Smolensk crash, apart from a poor condition of technical infrastructure at the Smolensk airport. It is, however, a deliberate idea of Kaczyński to use the valid elements of the analogy and then draw upon a long-standing anti-Russian sentiment, to blur any problems with the remaining element. The consequence is an implicit accusation of Russia of playing a role in the Smolensk catastrophe, yet more importantly, a possibility to openly criticize the non-believers for their "anti-Polish," unpatriotic views. Thus, eventually, the analogy comes to perform another act of moral exclusion of the "worst sort," just like the earlier strategies. We continue to discuss the role of analogies in L&J's discourse later on, in Section 4.2.

Meanwhile, it should be noted that the "worst sort narrative" goes way beyond issues of governance, national memory, and truth, drawing some further distinctions—more or less explicit—in relation to ecology, social activism, or even gender identity and sexual orientation. As for the latter, L&J's public discourse between 2015 and 2019 contains a number of examples of discriminatory, homophobic language directed at the LGBT community, in Poland and abroad. Deeply offensive language is directed, as well, toward supporters of the rights of LGBT groups, such as marital or even inheritance rights. Mizielińska and Stasińska (2017) view the political-pragmatic function of such a discourse as an attempt to cement L&J's control over the right wing of Polish politics. Apparently, in the course of the 2015–19 term, L&J's leaders strengthen their hold on traditional values, using LGBT issues to reinforce the loyalty of their conservative voters. Thus, LGBT itself is construed as an "ideology," rather than a community of people. For example, in an interview for TVP1 Prime Minister Morawiecki speaks of an "imported LGBT movement (. . .) that threatens our identity, our nation, its continued existence, and therefore the Polish state" (Mateusz Morawiecki, April 19, 2019). The term "imported" is particularly indicative here, as L&J's strategy is indeed to present LGBT as a *foreign* ideology in order to mobilize its electorate against what thus seems an "invasion." Krystyna Pawłowicz, one of the most outspoken figures of the L&J camp, says directly: "we must win this culture war" (press interview for Gazeta Polska, May 16, 2019). Construing the LGBT community discursively—through deictic othering and proximization—as a war invader goes a long way: it allows L&J to focus on the potential "victims." Interestingly enough, these are construed in physical, rather than ideological, terms. At a party convention on April 19, 2019, Jarosław Kaczyński declares: "This [LGBT] danger is an attack on the family, and an attack conducted in the worst possible way, because it's essentially an attack on children." He goes on to warn LGBT activists: "Keep your hands off our children. Sexualisation of children will be fought and defeated." Kaczyński's words are part of L&J's argument against the expansion of sex education in schools. Especially in recent time Law & Justice has argued that such classes are used by LGBT groups to "sexualise children" and even prepare them for abuse. As we can imagine, supporters of sex education programs emerge in such an argument as inherently evil, the real "worst sort" of people.

The concept of "attack on the family" underlies another hot social issue that L&J invokes regularly to bolster its support among the conservative electorate, namely, abortion. Notably, Poland has one of the harshest abortion laws in Europe, a relic of its Catholic revival after the fall of communism. Referred to as the "abortion compromise," the law is a result of pressure from the Roman Catholic Church, which played a seminal role in the fight against communism and has since held sway over those in power. Termination is allowed only when the fetus is malformed, the health or life of the mother is in jeopardy, or in the event of rape or incest. Even in these cases, however, abortions can be difficult to obtain as medical professionals have the right to invoke a clause that allows for conscientious objection (Cullen and Korolczuk 2019). Even though there is currently no serious political initiative to liberalize the aforementioned laws, Law & Justice invokes the issue of abortion fairly frequently, attributing such an intention to its parliamentary opposition, as well as grassroots movements and women's rights activists in general. Such organizations and their members are accused—in recent words by Kaczyński—of "implement[ing] foreign values that undermine Christian morality and teaching" (Jarosław Kaczyński for Gazeta Polska, June 2, 2019). This shows, just like the LGBT case, that in L&J's home-front discourse the construal of the internal adversary and the "worst sort" may involve visions of nearly political-conspiratory nature, bringing back memories as distant as the postwar years (see 2.1).

The way Law & Justice handles the LGBT and abortion matters reveals one of its favorite and apparently effective leadership strategies: a discursive ideologization of difficult and potentially controversial, yet essentially non-ideological, issues of the Polish public space to generate social conflict involving a clear political adversary. Once the ideological distinctions are clearly marked, L&J enacts leadership by, first, instilling an aura of threat from the adversary, and second, proposing countermeasures in line with conservative predispositions of its voters. The final example in this section is L&J's management of environmental issues, especially its stance on the pressure from the EU as well as climate organizations at home to slash emissions and reduce pollution by phasing out the use and production of coal. Coal generates about 80 percent of Poland's electricity and the industry employs about 150,000 people. This makes curbing the production a sensitive issue and a serious problem for the L&J government, which has made coal and coal miners an important part of its economic and political program. Clearly, the government is wary of alienating miners whose votes are needed to keep the party in power. It is thus slow to introduce transformation measures, as these would entail a massive reduction of jobs in the industry. On the other hand, the defense of coal has put L&J at loggerheads with Brussels and its Green Deal effort to make the continent climate-neutral by 2050 (Szulecka and Szulecki 2019).

To defend its inaction, the L&J government uses a quasi-patriotic discourse that makes coal and coal production an important issue of national sovereignty. The central argument is that own production of coal keeps away the threat of economic and thus also political dependency—mostly on Russia. This stance is expressed in PM Morawiecki's speech at a meeting of EU leaders: "Poland will reach climate neutrality at its own pace. Our climate transformation must be, first of all, *safe* for Poland" (Mateusz Morawiecki, May 13, 2019). This kind of argument is communicated against a broader social context and involves specific lexical choices. In particular, speaking about coal as Poland's natural resource, L&J reactivates sentiments and reinvokes visions that have been popular among Poles for decades. Namely, coal is construed as the land's precious and bountiful gift, and Polish miners are presented—again—as the nation's working-class heroes. For example, in his 2017 exposé, Morawiecki calls coal "the country's black gold," while referring to miners as "those who embody the very best of Poland." As one can imagine, it is hard to oppose such an argument—and thus L&J's coal policy in general—without earning the reputation of the "worst sort."

4.2. Historical Analogies and Temporal-Axiological Proximization

We have noted several times in this book that history plays a central role in L&J's discourse. Historical narratives designed by Kaczyński and other party leaders perform a number of socio-ideological and pragmatic functions. Typically, they define values, ideological beliefs, and postures relative to which social distinctions are drawn, marked linguistically, and enacted in discourse. A prominent example is the Round Table narrative, which, as we have observed, lies at the core of the distinction between the "solidarity" and "liberal" camps. Elsewhere, however, Law & Justice exploits Poland's history to establish conceptual analogies to endorse its political visions and, crucially, reject the competing or alternative visions. This is done by invoking difficult or plainly tragic historical events to draw parallels between the past actions that contributed to those events and the present postures and behaviors of L&J's political opponents. The goal is to present the adversaries as a politically irresponsible group, devoid of a sense of historical insight, ignoring "lessons of the past" and thus being a threat to the Polish raison d'état or even to Poland as a sovereign state. To realize this goal, L&J politicians make frequent use of emotionally charged power words that evoke immediate—and unequivocal—associations with the past events and their actors.

4.2.1. "Targowica" and "shmaltsovniks"

Among these historical catchwords, "Targowica" ranks without doubt as the number one choice in L&J's discourse, occurring as many as 958 times in the 2015–19 corpus. This means that it appears, on average, twice in a single text of the corpus—including speeches, press statements, media interviews, as well as short comments and remarks. The word "Targowica" refers historically to the Targowica Confederation, which was a confederation established by Polish and Lithuanian magnates on April 27, 1792, in Saint Petersburg, with the backing of the Russian Empress Catherine II. The confederation was launched to oppose some of the provisions of the Constitution of May 3 (which had been adopted a year before by the Great Sejm, that is, Parliament of the Polish-Lithuanian Commonwealth), particularly those limiting the privileges of the nobility. Although the objective of the confederates was essentially legislative and involving, most of all, restoration of the legal *status quo ante*, the political effects turned out disastrous. The involvement of Russia in drafting the founding act of the confederation led, with time, to political tensions and eventually to the Polish-Russian War of 1792. This in turn precipitated the Second Partition of Poland (the First took place in 1772) and set the stage for the Third Partition and the final dissolution of the Polish-Lithuanian Commonwealth in 1795. In consequence, Poland vanished from the map of Europe for the next 123 years, until the end of the First World War in 1918. As could be expected, the expression "Targowica" has gained ever since a highly pejorative meaning in Polish public discourse, functioning as a synonym of national treason (Leszczyński 2018).

The motif of treason associated with "Targowica" is extensively exploited in L&J's discourse, particularly to delegitimize attempts of the party's opponents to have European institutions (such as the European Commission and European Parliament) look into legality of reforms introduced by the ruling party into the judiciary. Since the beginning of L&J's rule in 2015, the opposition, both parliamentary and extra-parliamentary, called repeatedly on different EU bodies to review the ongoing sweeping reforms for their constitutionality as well as consistency with European law. These calls played a major role in EU's decision, in 2017, to have all the new regulations assessed by the Venice Commission,[9] which declared that a bulk of the new provisions were indeed unconstitutional and contradicting EU law. As virtually all of the subsequent suggestions and recommendations for amendments were disregarded by the L&J government, in November 2017 the European Parliament triggered in relation to Poland Article 7 of the Treaty on European Union (TEU). The Article involves a procedure under which certain rights from a member state can be suspended, as punishment for breaching (some of) the EU's founding values, such as respect for human dignity, freedom, democracy, equality, and—notably—the rule of law. The EP resolution regarding application of Article 7 was passed by a vast majority of votes, which included also the votes of fourteen Polish MEPs (some of whom were former members of the Civic Platform group in the Polish Parliament).

As could be expected, the 14 MEPs came under a massive attack from L&J politicians and the party's supporters at home, who did not hesitate to call them "traitors," "guided by a sense of servitude to foreign interests" (Jarosław Kaczyński for Gazeta Polska, November 30, 2017). The aftermath of the EP resolution was when the concept of "Targowica" was invoked most frequently, to delegitimize the opposition and simultaneously present the L&J government as the only guarantor of Poland's political sovereignty and raison d'état. Thus, L&J's discourse in late 2017 and early 2018 involving changes in the Polish judiciary and their reception abroad nearly always includes the image of a "foreign informer" acting in complete disregard of the state's interests. In this kind of discourse, "Targowica" is at the same time a conceptual and a linguistic construct:

(6) The EP resolution aims to endorse a second class membership of Poland in the EU. Its goal is to humiliate the Polish government and establish colonial dependence of Poland on international political organizations. The EP is not concerned about any reform but intends to fight the Polish government which is acknowledged to be an alien body within the EU. The EP resolution is thus another show of arrogance towards Poland (. . .) But let us not forget that this resolution would not have happened but for the shameful activity of Mrs. Pitera, Mrs. Kudrycka, Mr. Boni, Mrs. Hübner[10], judges such as Mr. Żurek and Mr. Tuleya,[11] and all those who in their life,

in their jobs and whatever they do, choose to inform on Poland rather than serve it. These people cannot be called anything other than denouncers and traitors, they are contemporary Targowica. (Foreign Minister Witold Waszczykowski, December 12, 2017)

In example (6), the reference to "Targowica" wraps up an argument that serves two main purposes. On the one hand, it explains, primarily to L&J voters, the reasons for what seems like a major crisis in the relations between Poland and the EU. This explanation is obviously necessary to keep legitimization of the L&J rule intact. However, apart from playing an explanatory and justification role, the argument aims to further strengthen the leadership, by construing an urgent domestic threat that needs a swift response. Thus, in Waszczykowski's comment, the foreign domain and the domestic domain are closely connected, forming a causative structure ("But let us not forget . . .") that contains a clearly demarcated *Them* camp. It is interesting to note that while the designation of the camp as a whole is clear and the lexical labels used are explicit enough ("denouncers and traitors"), the member entities of the camp are defined in various degrees of specificity. There are, of course, members that need to be pointed to directly, such as the four MEPs, as their mention serves to explain the crisis situation in the most efficient and politically beneficial way. However, there are also *Them* entities that are referred to generally as a class ("judges") or, finally, entities that are completely vague, such as "all those who in their life, in their jobs and whatever they do, choose to inform on Poland rather than serve it." The presence of the latter entities in the argument adds to the threat by making it less tangible and thus more difficult to handle. At the same time, the argument benefits rhetorically from the fact that the assertion of a threat that has no material outlines remains virtually undeniable. This makes the concept of "Targowica" invoked in the last line extend over and apply to a potentially infinite number of enemy entities, which can be identified in further texts according to current needs of their authors. Indeed, in most of their "Targowica discourse" following Waszczykowski's comment in November 2017, leaders of Law & Justice tend to use the concept to embrace a broad range of adversaries, in and beyond the domain of the judiciary (Leszczyński 2018).

The argument in (6) and its management of the Targowica concept is, also, a model example of the construal of historical analogy involving the use of temporal-axiological proximization in the service of mobilization and social coercion. The proximization is, on the one hand, axiological, in the sense that it involves conflation of a past event (setting up the Targowica Confederation) and a present event (the voting of the Polish group, together with other MEPs, for the implementation of Article 7), relative to ideological motives and the underlying values. These values are, following the line of Waszczykowski's argument, opportunism, selfishness, political irresponsibility, and a lack of historical insight. On the other hand, it is temporal, in the sense that the "past/source" values (defining the Confederation) are assigned, by principle of metaphor, to the "present/target" political actors (the fourteen Polish MEPs). The consequences of this conceptual projection are also twofold. First, the entire political agenda of the fourteen MEPs (and their home political environment opposing L&J's rule) gets automatically delegitimized as contrary to national interests. Furthermore, the future activity of the group emerges, under the circumstances, as a major political threat to Poland. The latter factor possesses a clear coercive value, mobilizing L&J voters in their continued support for the party and the government.

L&J's discourse of the late 2017 and early 2018 includes, apart from "Targowica," also other terms to describe (or malign, actually) people alerting European institutions to possible breaches of EU law in Poland. For instance, in an interview with the Polish Press Agency a prominent L&J politician, Ryszard Czarnecki, compares Róża Thun, a Polish parliamentary and civil rights activist, to "shmaltsovniks"—the infamous blackmailers who during the Second World War extorted money from Jews hiding from the German Nazis, by threatening to expose them:

> (7) During World War II we had shmaltsovniks, and today we have got Róża von Thun und Hohenstein and, unfortunately, she follows a certain tradition. Let us hope voters remember it and bill her for that when the time of voting comes. (Ryszard Czarnecki, February 7, 2018)

Czarnecki's words may sound outrageous, but in a bigger context his comment fits rhetorically very well into a default strategy of historical narration followed by Law & Justice from the very moment of coming to power in 2015. On this strategy, Poland is viewed (and presented) as a unique country, the "Messiah of nations" and "a defender of the Catholic faith in Europe" (Gomola 2019: 84–5). This kind of exceptionalism emerges, on a religious and cultural plane, out of the influence of Pope John Paul II (understood by the faithful to be the Vicar of Christ on Earth) and, on a political plane, from Solidarity's historical victory over the communist government in the 1989 elections. According to Kaczyński and other leaders of the party, being aided by God (via Pope John Paul II) and having successfully been the first country to defy Soviet influence and lead the way in shedding the chains of communism makes Poland entitled to an assertive presence in Europe and playing a key role in the EU (Gomola 2019). Even though the image of Poland is occasionally flawed by activity of groups of the "worst sort," these groups remain on the margins of society. The terms used to describe these groups are thus ones that suggest moral or ideological extremity—such as "Targowica" or "shmaltsovniks." These historical terms, virtually unused for decades, are now being revived and given a new life in public discourse, in order to perform one function, that is, exclude their referents from the national in-group as defined by the L&J party.

4.2.2. Ruling by Enmification

Understandably, one might wonder about the rationale for such radical discourse and the essentially offensive expressions. How do they manage to function in the public domain, constituting an integral part of language used by L&J politicians that is apparently accepted by voters? The research by Gerő et al. (2017) provides an interesting explanation based on transdisciplinary insights from social and political psychology. According to the authors, the politics of internal enemy-making—enmification—and the accompanying radicalization of discourse are among the most salient characteristics of post-totalitarian political systems, especially those having moved from the Soviet model of communism to democracy and neoliberal economy. While the fall of the Soviet bloc meant an increase in hope for the blooming of a multitude of possible social, economic, and political logics in the region (Shields 2012), the historical legacy of Central and Eastern Europe, combined with its geopolitical context and its historical path dependency, has led to the establishment of a specific political and economic model whose societies might be described as "hypercapitalist" or "over-privatized" (Jacobsson 2015). Since no sufficient adjustment to neoliberal policies in these societies has ever occurred, social inequalities have become deeper and economic disparity endures. This results, even in states with relatively "healthy" economic indicators such as Poland, in a high level of individual stress and social frustration, which generates a response. A common response is, argue Gerő et al. (2017), raising one's own status against the odds by finding a scapegoat, an internal enemy to whom blame for economic problems and failures can be allocated. Political actors exploit this tendency, by seeking out and proposing discursive tools and terms to express the hostility and antagonism, in a way that simultaneously cements the loyalty of voters.

Furthermore, Gerő et al. (2017) demonstrate that enmification is firmly linked with fear generation and coercion. When people perceive threats (which they see directly or which are communicated to them), they activate a regressive defense mechanism that "switches off" certain functions of the mind that are responsible for critical thinking and the sustaining of individual autonomy (Volkan 1985). They develop a strong collective identity, engaging with the group (social or political) they consider their own. Most crucially, they expect the leader or leaders of the group to contain the threat, and are happy to accept extraordinary and often radical means that are used to do so. These means may be physical or discursive, or involving both actions and highly performative and appealing discourse forms, such as blaming or scapegoating.

Gerő et al.'s (2017) study goes a long way toward explaining the rhetorical effectiveness of the "worst sort," "Targowica," "shmaltsovniks," and other hard-hitting enmification terms in L&J's discourse. Most of these terms are hardly sophisticated and generally easy to grasp and circulate, which makes them travel further through different propagandistic channels of communication, often with the help of the state media. Importantly, being predominantly single-word or single-phrase expressions, they are readily extractable from larger discourse and easily entextualizable in a new piece of text. Thus, much of L&J's leadership rhetoric relies for its success on parties that recompose and subsequently redistribute the original information and propaganda messages at various levels of central and local government, and their media. This explains, in fact, several recent policies and actions of the ruling party that aim at gaining more control over local government structures as well as local press outlets (Wylęgalski 2019).

4.3. Insights from the Balkans: The Roma Case

The account of L&J's enmification strategies in terms of Gerő et al.'s (2017) research deriving from historical and geopolitical considerations leads to the question of whether internal enmification occurs in other Central and Eastern European societies and their discourses. Intriguingly enough, the politics of internal enemy-making seems virtually absent from ethnically homogeneous countries comparable to Poland. It occurs, however, in multiethnic societies in countries such as Slovakia, Romania, Bulgaria, and Hungary, where right-wing political forces often use the discursive strategies of self-justification, blaming and scapegoating in the way similar to L&J politicians. The most notable cases are, apparently, Bulgaria and Romania, where the aforementioned accusatory strategies are targeted against the Roma minority. Specifically, some political groups "construct" Romas as a distinct and problematic (socially, politically, and economically) entity inhabiting the state, yet separate from the nation (McGarry 2017: 11).

In their study of the linguistic-discursive manifestations of "Romaphobia" across Europe, Kaneva and Popescu (2014) attribute the situation in Bulgaria and Romania to what they call "a general rise of anti-Roma attitudes" and "a silent acceptance by many societies to denigrate Roma by invoking negative so-called traits and characteristics which all Roma supposedly possess, such as criminality, deviancy, and living parasitic lifestyles" (: 26). Thus, Romaphobia is manifest in the hate speech articulated by the Interior Minister for Italy, Matteo Salvini, who has called for ethnic profiling of Roma; in the attacks by neo-Nazis in Ukraine destroying homes and killing innocent Roma; and in the forced eviction of 8,161 Roma from their homes by French authorities in 2017 (McGarry 2017). It is present, argue Kaneva and Popescu (2014), in casual conversations in homes and at work, in media portrayals of the stereotypical carnivalesque Gypsy, in the town planners' placing of Roma in ghettos, or when authorities accuse Roma of abducting blond-haired, blue-eyed children. According to the authors, Romaphobia is "the last acceptable form of racism" (: 28), performing a specific sociopsychological function. This function is, as has been noted, scapegoating and blame assignment.

Exploring historical and anthropological contexts and underlying causes of the modern Romaphobia, McGarry (2017) concludes that the key to understanding why Roma are marginalized and stigmatized lies—interestingly enough—in our conception of territory and space, as well as processes of identity construction and maintenance. The most prominent example of this identity work is the stereotype of Roma as itinerant "nomads" who have no home or fixed roots, which serves to justify their exclusion today. In other words, nowhere are Roma regarded as belonging, as "one of us." As a nation without a territory, Roma do not fit any conception of nationalism, as every such conception equates one nation with one sovereign territory. As a result, Roma are excluded from public life and are seen as a problem community that do not "fit" the projection of the nation. This in turn makes them ideal scapegoats of the state (McGarry 2017).

The research of McGarry (2017) and Kaneva and Popescu (2014) demonstrates that the status of Roma as an internal *Them* entity derives from different factors than the analogical status of social or political "worst sort" groups in an ethnically homogeneous country such as Poland. At the same time, however, the discursive mechanisms and practices and, crucially, the political aims and benefits of enmification seem quite similar, as the following examples clearly indicate. In November 2017, the district court of the Bulgarian city of Burgas found the country's deputy PM Valeri Simeonov guilty of hate speech toward Bulgaria's Roma minority. Simeonov was convicted over an address he made in the Bulgarian parliament earlier that year (McGarry 2017). In the address, he described the Bulgarian Roma as "wild, arrogant, presumptuous and ferocious humanoids, demanding wages without labor, demanding sick-leave benefits without being sick, child benefits for children that play outside with the street-pigs, and maternity benefits for women with the instincts of street bitches." He went on to blame Roma for the country's dwindling economic growth and, eventually, for hampering negotiations over EU funds by "tarnishing the image of hard-working Bulgarians." Valeri Simeonov is the leader of National Front for the Salvation of Bulgaria (NFSB), a party whose founding manifesto[12] considers Roma a major internal threat to the social as well as economic well-being of Bulgarians. It envisages the dispersal of what it calls "Gypsy ghettos," and isolating Roma in closed "reservations," according to the model of Native American or Indigenous Australian reservations. Harrowing as such views and proposals definitely are, neither the party nor Simeonov himself was ever held accountable—until 2017.

Still, despite the Burgas court ruling, the process of enmification of the Roma minority by a number of significant political groups in Bulgaria shows no signs of abating. Most recently, there have been voices from the radical right blaming Roma for difficulties in fighting the Covid-19 pandemic in Bulgaria. For example, in an interview with BNT Novini, the news channel of the Bulgarian National Television, MEP Angel Dzhambazki called for

Roma neighborhoods in Bulgaria to be closed during the pandemic, stating that "Gypsies have a very low health culture" and "have no personal hygiene." Asked by the journalist to elaborate, he added the following: "If you leave the gypsies free to walk up and down and probably spread the infection, it is mild to say ill-advised, mild to say irregular, mild to say beyond any logic. Gypsies are engaged in begging, theft and prostitution."[13] Views such as Dzhambazki's cannot be taken as representative of the full political spectrum in Bulgaria, but they are by no means marginal, either. Indeed, particularly during the time of the pandemic, the Roma minority has become an easy social target and entity addressed strategically in public discourse to solicit support for various policies and political projects.

There is a telling example from Romania that represents a case of such strategic enmification involving much-evocative multimodal ploys. Embracing the global spirit of commercialization and mediatization, Romania has developed since EU accession in 2007 a penchant for deploying government-sponsored branding campaigns in main national newspapers to "defend" its national identity against unflattering foreign representations (Kaneva and Popescu 2014). A rather sinister manifestation of the Romanian government's obsession with dispelling foreigners' ignorance about Romania—and their presumed inability to tell apart "real" Romanians from Roma—was a "Romanians in Europe" poster campaign run in the years 2012–13. The aim of the campaign was, in the words of the then–Prime Minister Mihai Ungureanu, to "promote a correct image of Romania in Europe and eliminate any confusion between 'Roma' and 'Romanians.'"[14] One poster from the campaign, published in *Jurnalul Național*, is particularly striking.[15] The poster displays two photos of "Roma" and "Romanians" placed side by side. The "Roma" photo, on the left, features two men, five women of varying ages but clearly younger than the men, and a baby. All are standing or squatting next to a wire fence, in front of a low-cost, concrete apartment building. They are dressed in brightly colored, garish clothing; the men wear hats and all but one of the women wear headscarves. Their skin is visibly darker than the skin of "Romanians" in the other photo. The "Romanian" photo shows a family of five—father, mother, two boys, and a girl—seated against a blue studio background, facing the camera directly and smiling cheerfully. They are all blond, have fair complexion, and are dressed in immaculate white shirts and blue jeans. The poster includes a "legend." The left photo is pointed to by a black arrow containing a text that reads, "Those people are Roma." By contrast, the right photo is pointed to by a yellow-blue-red (colors of the Romanian flag) arrow reading, "Those people are Romanians." Above the two photos runs a text in large block capitals: "Notice the difference!" Finally, a caption underneath the photos explains: "Roma and Romanians are two different peoples."

Compared to the examples from Bulgaria, the aforementioned Romanian case of enmification may look "softer," amounting, at least at first sight, to a case of "othering," rather than enmification per se. After all, while voices such as Simeonov's or Dzhambazki's emerge as openly accusatory and denigrating, discursive strategies used in the "Romanians in Europe" campaign seem to "only" invoke, or reflect, the (already) existing ethnic distinctions. They do not blame, denigrate, accuse, and so on; nor do they construe any direct threats. However, there are clear analogies at other important levels, involving motivation and political benefits. In that regard, both cases represent discursively performed attempts at reinforcing, as well as constructing, firm social divisions within a country, in the interest of a broader policy legitimization and potentially stronger leadership. This is particularly striking in the Romanian example, where the government has chosen to "sacrifice," in a sense, a part of the society, with a view to envisage global benefits such as a friendlier(?) image and quicker EU integration.

Taken together, the examples of internal othering and enmification from Bulgaria and Romania reveal both differences and similarities to the "worst sort" discourse introduced by the Law & Justice party in Poland. On the one hand, the enmification terms and strategies in the two Balkan countries draw upon long-existing social distinctions and the resulting conflicts, which, as we noted before, do not occur in ethnically homogeneous states such as Poland. On the other hand, though, the discursive construction of the "worst sort" groups by the ruling party in Poland is, at linguistic as well as the underlying social and political levels, remarkably similar to the construction of Roma communities by leading political forces in Bulgaria in Romania. Most notably, in both cases, the construal of the intranational *Them* draws upon a conceptual distinction between "nation" and "state." Forcing this distinction as the main criterion for social affiliation, top political actors in the three countries construe their sociopolitical adversaries as "problematic" entities, which, in McGarry's (2017) words, "inhabit the state" yet remain "separate from the nation" (: 11). In Poland, such derogatory labels, put on different groups of political opposition, are often—as we have noted—the result of the practice that L&J politicians describe as "informing on Poland" to EU institutions. This motif will return several times in the next two chapters, where we explore the international dimension of L&J's policy and discourse.

5

European Union and the Discourse of National Sovereignty

In this chapter we move the focus of analysis of L&J's discourse from its home arena to the domain of international relations, particularly Poland's relations with the European Union. We have noted in the previous chapter that the first term of the L&J government (2015–19) reveals a rich history of crises and conflicts between Warsaw and Brussels, which are both reflected in as well as created and then perpetuated by discourse. The present chapter identifies and explores two principal areas in which these conflicts and mutual animosities arise. The first is the issue of migration and the stance of Law & Justice on EU immigration policy to handle the unprecedented migration crisis in Europe continuing since 2015. Over the years 2015–19 and in fact until now (2020), the L&J government has vehemently refused to honor the EU refugee relocation agenda agreed on by the former (CP) government in May 2015. The second conflict area is, as noted in Chapter 4, L&J's complete overhaul of the judiciary in Poland, which has been criticized and formally opposed by EU institutions—such as the EU Commission and the European Parliament—eventually resulting in implementation of Article 7 of the EU treaty.

The discussion in the chapter shows that the L&J government draws on the two conflict domains to construct a specific kind of discourse, which can be termed the discourse of "national sovereignty." While the sovereignty discourse is developed in relation to international, mostly European, issues, its principal target group remains the Polish political audience comprising mainly L&J voters. Intrinsically connected to Kaczyński's conception of state legitimacy and political and economic security, which we discussed earlier (cf. 3.1; 4.1), the sovereignty discourse of L&J has the primary goal of enacting strong and effective leadership, which guarantees people's safety notwithstanding the ominous presence of a serious external threat. The chapter demonstrates that in this kind of discourse threats are construed as less or more direct and tangible, extending over Poland seen as a sovereign state (political threats) and simultaneously over Poland understood as a nation (ideological threats). For example, threats to the country resulting from the migration crisis and abiding by relocation schemas proposed by the EU involve, in L&J's sovereignty discourse, the direct threat to security caused by the influx of foreigners representing different cultures, ideologies, and religions, as well as a threat of political subordination to Brussels.

In its comparative dimension, the discourse of national sovereignty developed by Law & Justice in the 2015–19 term reveals a striking number of analogies and genuinely fascinating similarities to the discourse of the 2016 Brexit referendum in the UK. Particularly, in its conceptual, pragmatic, and lexical construction, it clearly follows up on the rhetoric of the United Kingdom Independence Party (UKIP), urging the British (successfully, as we know now) to leave the European Union. Moreover, many anti-EU speeches by Kaczyński bear some hard-to-miss discursive similarities with the then-leader of the UKIP, Nigel Farage. Finally, the UKIP and L&J discourses meet most conspicuously on issues of refugee crisis and EU policy on immigration.[1] These observations determine the structure of the chapter. In its first part, we explore, in comparative as well as contrastive terms, the UKIP's Brexit discourse and L&J's national sovereignty discourse, tackling some obviously emerging questions about the future political consequences of the latter.[2] In the second part, we look at discursive strategies whereby L&J construes EU response to the L&J government's reform of the Polish judiciary in terms of an illegitimate foreign intervention and thus—again—a threat to Poland's political sovereignty. The analysis includes, among others, Warsaw's formal (diplomatic) reactions to the implementation, against Poland, of Article 7 of the EU treaty. While this issue was initially addressed in the previous chapter, our current interest is in international communication, rather than the "worst sort" and other discourses developed mostly for the home addressee.

5.1. Immigration and Sovereignty: From Brexit to . . . Polexit?

As has been observed, a crucial reason to compare L&J's sovereignty discourse with the Brexit rhetoric of the UKIP during the referendum campaign is the essentially negative stance of both parties on policies proposed by the EU to handle the gathering migration crisis in Europe. Another important similarity involves the way in which the question of immigration is tied discursively to the global issues of national sovereignty and democracy. In this regard, the discourse of Jarosław Kaczyński and other L&J politicians seems at places a true copy of anti-European, isolationist, and often plainly xenophobic voices developing in Britain before the 2016 referendum. It is worth taking a longer look at how these initially random voices had turned over time into established discourses, affecting the outcome of the referendum and thus becoming—ever since—proven rhetorical models for conservative Eurosceptic groups and parties across Europe.

5.1.1. Farage's Rhetoric of Exceptionalism and Isolation

While the discourse that frames migration into Britain as a threat to British people's sense of security and the country's sovereignty is rightly associated with the UKIP's leader Nigel Farage, the origins of this discourse can be found before the beginning of the referendum campaign. As noted by Tournier-Sol (2017), isolationist positions drawing on issues of immigration and identity differences emerge in many public appearances of leaders of the ruling Conservative party in the early 2010s, including the then–Prime Minister David Cameron. A lucid example is Cameron's speech at Bloomberg on January 23, 2013, in which he invokes concepts of the European Union, national sovereignty, and democracy, making an explicit link between British identity and foreign policy:

> (1) I know that the United Kingdom is sometimes seen as an argumentative and rather strong-minded member of the family of European nations. And it's true that our geography has shaped our psychology. We have the character of an island nation—independent, forthright, passionate in defence of our sovereignty. We can no more change this British sensibility than we can drain the English Channel. And because of this sensibility, we come to the European Union with a frame of mind that is more practical than emotional. For us, the European Union is a means to an end—prosperity, stability, the anchor of freedom and democracy both within Europe and beyond her shores—not an end in itself. (David Cameron at Bloomberg, January 23, 2013)

Later in the speech, Cameron goes on to note that "there is a gap between the EU and its citizens which has grown dramatically in recent years. And which represents a lack of democratic accountability and consent that is felt particularly acutely in Britain." He affirms that "there is a growing frustration that the EU is regarded as something that is done to people rather than acting on their behalf" and that "democratic consent for the EU in Britain is now wafer thin." This leads him to conclude that "we [the people of the EU] need to have a bigger and more significant role for national parliaments. There is not, in my view, a single European demos. It is national parliaments, which are and will remain the true source of democratic legitimacy and accountability in the EU" (Cameron 2013).

These excerpts show David Cameron advocating British exceptionalism and enacting a strong political distinction by reference to an "independent" and "forthright" country that is an "island nation." Cameron rejects the notion of "a single European self" and prioritizes national parliaments, thereby privileging the "national self" and rejecting a shared sense of European identity. In the long run this implies that any act performed in the interest of "Europe" is potentially anti-British and can be considered a threat (Todd 2015). Altogether, Cameron's Bloomberg speech sets the terms for the debate over the rest of 2013 and in fact the entire period preceding the referendum (Todd 2015). Conservative backbenchers take his arguments further still, often arguing for a defense of British sovereignty through reference to history and especially the Second World War. Richard Shepherd (Conservative) asserts that:

> (2) This [referendum] vote, what we decide and what people in the future decide will determine the character and strength of our national constitutional history, which is being threatened. Why should we defer in such an adventure, when this is the most remarkable and ancient of all the democratic communities within western Europe? Why? (Hansard 2013–14: 1201)

Shepherd's argument is elaborated on by another Conservative, William Cash, who refers to Churchill and Britain's war sacrifice:

> (3) People have fought and died. The only reason we live in the United Kingdom in peace and prosperity is because, in the second and first world wars, we stood up for that freedom and democracy. Churchill galvanised the British people to stand up for the very principles that are now at stake. It is

inconceivable that only 30 years after the end of the second world war, the British people would have willingly embarked on a programme to hand over swathes of their hard-won sovereignty to another state, and let us be clear: that is what the European Union aspires to be. (Hansard 2013–14: 1232)

The geopolitical and historical references by David Cameron and his Conservative colleagues serve to consolidate the national self. They stress the centrality of the moment and prescribe the future course of action. The historical flashbacks in texts (2) and (3) activate a specific kind of reasoning based on the principle of analogy. On this logic, political legitimacy and the mandate to rule are defined and assessed by their consistency with historically accepted principles and solutions (Musolff 2016). The past is thus treated as a lesson to heed into an uncertain future.

In retrospect, the ideological discourse of members of the ruling Conservative party a few years before the Brexit referendum seems to constitute, somewhat ironically, much of the groundwork on which the UKIP and Nigel Farage develop, later on, their increasingly radical anti-European rhetoric. From the very beginning of his campaign for the Leave vote, Farage organizes the main parts of his argument, just like Cameron, around identity issues:

(4) The fact is we just don't belong in the European Union. Britain is different. Our geography puts us apart. Our history puts us apart. Our institutions produced by that history put us apart. We think differently. We behave differently. (. . .) The roots go back seven, eight, nine hundred years with the Common Law. Civil rights. Habeas corpus. The presumption of innocence. The right to a trial by jury. On the continent confession is the mother of all evidence. (Nigel Farage at the UKIP autumn conference, September 19, 2013)

Farage's argument in (4) initiates a number of strategies that are going to appear throughout most of his 2013–16 discourse, getting increasingly salient and radical as the referendum date draws near. Specifically, he sets up a firm *Us*-vs.-*Them* distinction, which involves consistent deictic othering of the *Them* group, based on insurmountable historical and ideological differences. He appeals to the weight of "seven, eight, nine hundred years" of history, in which Great Britain is "different [from continental Europe]." He also addresses ethical dimensions of identity to differentiate between a British tradition of presumption of innocence and jury trial from a continental system based on confession. In the same speech Farage goes on to affirm that "[British people] know that only by leaving the Union [they] can regain control of [their] borders, [their] parliament, democracy and [their] ability to trade freely with the fastest-growing economies in the world." Implying lack of control of the "[UK] borders," he sets up a direct link to the immigration theme, framing it as an issue of extreme urgency and consequentiality. Like Cameron and his MPs, he employs identity and cultural differentiation (Todd 2015) to serve his political cause of increasing UKIP's electoral strength and achieving a British exit from the EU. The text in (4) is, altogether, an example of how Farage's rhetoric builds on the general aura of Euroscepticism observable right at the outset of the proto-referendum debate. The later discourse of the UKIP becomes gradually more distinctive; it makes the central arguments far more salient, unveiling specific rhetorical patterns and recurrent linguistic-pragmatic strategies.

Thus, in the years 2014–16 Farage's speeches establish immigration as the core issue and the primary argument used by the UKIP to make their case for the Leave vote. In this new and essentially coercive discourse, proximization emerges as the main conceptual tool and rhetorical strategy to construe the influx of immigrants in terms of a developing "*Them*-invasion." This can be seen from the following examples (5–8), which demonstrate the growing radicalism of Farage's stance in the 2014–16 period. Analytically, they fall into two pairs, (5–6) and (7–8), illustrating, respectively, two phases of the UKIP's discourse in the Brexit campaign (see Cap 2019).[3] In the first phase (examples 5–6), the coercive elements of Farage's rhetoric such as fear appeals can be described as relatively moderate:

> **(5)** In the last ten years opinion polls have shown substantial majorities in favour of cutting immigration to a rate at which it can be comfortably absorbed. Yet instead of listening to those who elected them, the government takes orders from the European Union and is throwing open our borders to more than 30 million Bulgarians and Romanians who may be coming to settle here. (. . .) What do we call it if not yet another sovereignty-sapping power grab from EU elites? And with our sovereignty and identity at stake, the time to act is now. I mean, the time has come to defy Brussels and declare that our country is full up. (Nigel Farage at the UKIP spring conference, February 28, 2014)

> **(6)** Truth is, in scores of our cities and market towns, this country in a short space of time is becoming unrecognisable. What I am saying is we now have

nearly 10 per cent of our schools in this country where English is not the primary language of the homes those children come from. And further, Migration Watch estimates that over 250,000 people from Bulgaria, the EU's poorest country, may be arriving over the next five years. Under EU rules, we are powerless to deny them entry or benefits after restrictions were lifted in January [2014]. If we don't re-claim our powers from Brussels, we risk losing control not only of our country's borders, our identity, but also the welfare state. (Nigel Farage at the European Parliament, May 25, 2014)

In examples (5–6), *Them* comprises mostly economic migrants from new member states of the EU such as Bulgaria and Romania. In ideological terms, *Them* applies also to "Brussels," as the promoter of free flow of people and the freedom of employment within the EU. This designation makes (5) and (6) quite moderate in their fear-inducing and coercive appeal—although a possibility is left for threat levels to rise in the future ("If we don't re-claim our powers from Brussels. . ."). Such an arrangement involves a balanced use of different proximization strategies. While spatial proximization is used to construe the ongoing arrival of migrants from the new member states in physical terms, axiological proximization is applied to construe some long-term consequences of immigration. These are conceptualized in largely socio-ideological terms, as a threat to sovereignty and national identity ("our sovereignty and identity at stake," "we risk losing control not only of our country's borders, our identity"). The axiological aspect of proximization in the two texts covers not only migrants, but also the "EU elites" in Brussels, who are held responsible for enforcing "sovereignty-sapping" policies against some of the countries' national interests. The argument in (6) makes explicit one of such interests, namely, the "welfare state." This phrase marks, incidentally, an important theme of the UKIP and Farage's immigration discourse (as well as, later, L&J's discourse in Poland), which can be described as "welfare chauvinism." Coined by Andersen and Bjørklund (1990), the term "welfare chauvinism" involves the perspective that state support should be restricted to national citizens and not provided to "others."

At pragmalinguistic and lexical levels, the proximization strategies in (5) and (6) comprise a variety of tools. First of all, much of the narration makes use of progressive tense forms. This pertains to both spatial and axiological proximization. The progressive aspect increases the appeal of the envisaged physical impact ("30 million Bulgarians and Romanians may be coming to settle here," "250,000 people (...) may be arriving over the next five years"), as well as strengthens identity-related claims and threats ("this country in a short space of time is becoming unrecognisable"). As noted in Cap (2019), the use of the progressive helps construe a negative scenario by conflating the present and the future. Namely, it describes a current developing event that presages an ominous future. Such a scenario, involving temporal proximization, derives extra strength from the strategic vagueness it carries, especially when specific modalities are used in support. As can be seen from (5) and (6), the encroachment threat has feeble temporal underpinnings and thus the apparent impossibility to determine the very moment or critical culmination of impact ("may be coming," "may be arriving") makes that threat bigger and harder to contain (Dunmire 2011). At the same time, the conflation of the present and the (ominous) future exerts coercion by centralizing the present timeframe as *the* moment to act preventively.

As the proximization strategies in texts (5) and (6) involve temporal projections and anticipations of the future, they are accompanied by rhetorical ploys whose goal is to earn credibility for the envisaged scenarios. Thus, the argument in (6) employs the strategy of "source-tagging." As has been mentioned in Chapter 1 (cf. 1.3.) source-tagging is a judgment attribution strategy whereby an authorial voice is invoked to communicate sensitive or controversial information (Groom 2000). By referring to research of the Migration Watch think tank, Farage endorses his threatening vision of mass migration from the new member states of the EU, legitimizing the urgent need for preventive measures. The criticality of the moment is graphically expressed in the last phrase in (5) ("our country is full up"), which includes a conceptual metaphor to strengthen its pragmatic appeal.

The other pair of examples (7–8) illustrates the second phase of Farage's Brexit rhetoric (years 2015–16[4]), which sees a considerable rise in threat levels (see also Cap 2019):

(7) Mr. Cameron and his ministers have chosen to duck questions about the scale of a new wave of immigration from Syria and other countries of the Middle East and North Africa. Today, *The Sun* reveals the shocking figure that nearly one in five of all rape or murder suspects is a non-EU migrant. The sheer scale of crimes committed by immigrants is astonishing. Confront our government with this embarrassing statistic and they try to get off the hook by talking about "context." So here's some context for that

crime figure. A report published today shows that, because of a loophole in the immigration rules, more than 20,000 migrants from outside the EU come to live here every year. It doesn't take a genius to work out that the two figures might be connected. (Nigel Farage at the European Parliament, September 9, 2015)

(8) We refuse to sacrifice our freedom and security for political correctness. We must call things by their true names. Rather than shedding tears like Federica Mogherini or organizing marches that solve nothing, the state should ensure the safety of its citizens. (. . .) To those who are happy to welcome immigrants at our doors, I have a suggestion: go and see the refugee camps in Turkey. See the gangs and the riots. See the young Muslim criminals. See the anger, violence, and terror. It is there and is ready for export. This kind of evil might not have reached us yet, but it is well in sight. And there is no-one in Brussels who can protect us when it comes. (Nigel Farage at BBC station, July 17, 2016)

In this second phase, *Them* is reconstrued to include non-EU migrants, especially Muslim immigrant groups from the Middle East and North Africa. This change allows for a swift radicalization of the UKIP's isolationist rhetoric, which now builds on the aura of fear triggered by the concurrent terrorist attacks and other criminal acts involving Islamic perpetrators. Hence, the argument in (8) involves an ominous threat construed by reference to the July 2016 terrorist attack in Nice. At the same time, it expresses a harsh critique of the passivity and lack of response from the EU ("Rather than shedding tears like Federica Mogherini [EU Foreign Minister] or organizing marches that solve nothing, the state should ensure the safety of its citizens").[5] Finally, comments such as (7) put a big question mark over everyday safety of the British people. The mention in (7) of "a new wave of immigration from Syria and other countries of the Middle East and North Africa" is thus essentially an act of warning (cf. Cap 2019: 77).

The strongest fear appeal in the two texts occurs in the narrative that develops in the second part of (8) (from "To those who are happy" until the end of the excerpt). This narrative demonstrates a peculiar discursive structure, involving a causative connection between two consecutively occurring segments, which can be described as "abstract/ideological" and "material/physical," respectively. The first segment ("refugee camps in Turkey (. . .) gangs and the riots (. . .) young Muslim criminals (. . .) anger, violence, and terror. It is there and is ready for export") provides sociopsychological context and conditions for emergence of a *Them* threat. The second segment ("This kind of evil might not have reached us yet, but it is well in sight") "updates," in a sense, the status of this threat, from a "remote possibility" to "actual occurrence" within the US space ("is well in sight"). Such a construal employs both axiological and spatiotemporal proximization. While the former involves the conceptualization of a distant vision derived from a specific ideological context, the latter turns that threatening vision into a tangible threat whose materialization is virtually inevitable ("when it comes"). The crucial lexico-grammatical element enacting this conceptual shift is thus the modal structure of the narrative, which includes a *might*-phrase ("might not have reached us yet") to establish a possibility and then a *be*-phrase ("is well in sight") to change that possibility into a fact. We will see this intriguing mechanism return in a full shape in L&J's anti-immigration discourse in Poland.

Meanwhile, it should be noted that a bulk of the UKIP and Farage's anti-immigration discourse in the referendum campaign reveals an extensive use of metaphor, particularly conceptual metaphors, which provide extra strength to the appeal of threat patterns enacted by proximization shifts (Cap 2019). This is hardly surprising since, as we have seen before (Sections 1.4.2; 3.2), metaphor and proximization are fundamentally connected with regard to conceptualization patterns arising in discourse space (cf. 1.4). The deictic center, a "home camp" of *Us* entities, is frequently conceptualized in/through discourse as a CONTAINER, thus othering the non-members, which are construed as foreign *Them* entities. As a result, metaphorization of the *Us* entities as elements of the CONTAINER provides for some excellent rhetorical benefits, especially in fear-generating and coercive discourses. In such discourses, threats to the CONTAINER and the *Us* elements derive from a limited volume of the CONTAINER and its inability to hold external entities, that is, *Them*, which gather in the process of proximization. Other benefits of metaphors recruiting the CONTAINER schema involve, as we have seen, the ability of CONTAINER, as a concept, to enter in complex patterns of understanding based on embodied experience—conceptual scenarios. Within these mental patterns, the scenarios—such as STATE IS CONTAINER or POLITICS IS WAR (cf. 3.2)—endorse some seemingly self-evident conclusions and further the resulting "natural" and "obvious" actions or solutions proposed by the speaker. Endowed with these features, the STATE IS CONTAINER metaphor has a long tradition in the British immigration discourse, in which it draws on the CONTAINER schema to conceptualize the country (Charteris-Black 2005). Hart (2010) presents evidence that metaphoric expressions construing the UK as a CONTAINER are a stable feature of the British discourse on immigration, reflecting an underlying cognitive arrangement, that is, perception of Britain as an island (see also our discussion of the theory of political metaphor in Section 1.4.2).

In Farage's anti-immigration discourse the CONTAINER metaphor involves some default lexical items reflecting and reinforcing the containment schema, such as "wave [of immigration]," "absorb," "throw open," "borders," "full up," and "burst." Their function is to construe a scenario that justifies a restrictive immigration policy to contain what is conceptualized as a growing political, social, and economic threat. The scenario comprises a structured set of inferences, such as the following:

- The country—Britain—has a limited capacity.
- Continued immigration could cause the country (the "container") to "burst."
- Immigration will continue as, "under orders from the EU," the government are "throwing open" the country's "borders."
- The country is thus under a real and growing threat to its national sovereignty.
- The only way to offset the threat is to force the government to ignore the "orders" and maintain a strict immigration policy.

The final inference ("to force the government to ignore the 'orders' ") is a direct instruction for the Brexit vote. The entire chain of inferences draws on the conventionality of the CONTAINER metaphor, which facilitates a swift reception of the conveyed insight. Farage's discourse includes also other reception facilitators, grounded in some further features of the CONTAINER schema. As noted by Chilton (2004: 88), the CONTAINER metaphor entails *exclusivity* such that members have to be *in* or *out* and that it entails "protection by means of exclusion," as opposed to any other means that are available to human societies. This makes people adapt to the reality construed through the CONTAINER metaphor on account of their territorial instinct and in-group allegiance (Jowett and O'Donnell 1992). Since, under the CONTAINER schema, the entity perceived as "container" is presupposed to cover a given territory and those inside the container are presupposed to own the territory it covers, the metaphor reinforces the general aura of stability and permanence associated with that entity (Musolff 2016: 25–38). This is why metaphors conceptualizing countries in terms of bounded entities are so ubiquitous in political discourse, particularly in immigration discourse. Thus, in Farage's Brexit rhetoric metaphors recruiting the CONTAINER schema surface widely toward the end of the referendum campaign:

> **(9)** We already have a problem with home grown terror. The last thing we need to do is add to it from the outside. We see the terrible mistakes that Germany and France have made over the course of the last couple of years. Mercifully, we are not part of the Schengen Area. Still, day in and day out we face waves of asylum seekers from Calais and Cherbourg, France's biggest ports. This only means that illegal entrants are already at our gates and we must stand firm because Britain is full to bursting point. The Government's own figures show that the UK has the highest levels of immigration in its history: in the last ten years, over two millions were added to the UK population, and the flow shows no signs of slowing. There are reports that say we're better off with mass immigration. But to me, there is an issue here called the quality of life and I think that matters more than money. Cause, I am getting a bit tired of my kids coming home from school being taught about every other religion in the world, celebrating every other religious holiday but not actually being taught about Christianity. Cause, I would remind you, of the eight people who committed those atrocities in Paris a mere three months ago,[6] five of them had got into Europe posing as refugees. So, there is an issue here. (Nigel Farage at the UKIP spring conference, February 29, 2016)

Made at the end of February 2016, Farage's address in (9) can be described as directly instrumental in shaping people's attitudes on the eve of the referendum. The argument includes several explicit fear appeals, involving ideological and physical threats. This duality is reflected in the two final sentences of the text, which construe, respectively, an identity threat and a material threat of terrorist attacks similar to the Paris attacks three months before. The job of preparing such a hard-hitting ending is performed by metaphors, which develop a convincing argument outlining the context of the growing threat. Thus, the first part of the text includes numerous lexical items and phrases depicting the impact of immigration ("*waves* of asylum seekers," "*flow* [with] no signs of slowing"), as well as the criticality of the home camp's condition ("illegal entrants are already at our *gates* and we must *stand firm* because Britain is *full* to *bursting* point," italics added). In this argument, the items engaged in construction of the CONTAINER metaphor are usually also markers of proximization (especially spatial proximization). The interplay of conceptual metaphor and proximization can be further noticed in the use of a historical flashback to generate analogy. Namely, the memory of "atrocities in Paris" is invoked and temporally proximized as a lesson to heed in the future. While Farage's 2013–16 discourse features, generally, a moderate number of such analogies, their occurrences increase visibly in the years 2015–16, as the referendum date draws near.

Altogether, Farage's (anti-)immigration discourse in the UKIP's Brexit campaign can be characterized as conceptually bipolar, recognizing the *Us/Them* distinction, and enacting this distinction with regard to identity, ideological, and policy issues. In the course of time, it expresses, first, relatively moderate positions, assuming a more radical stance in the years 2015–16. This change is both caused by and reflected in the change of Farage's focus, which moves over time from EU immigration to mostly Middle East and North African immigration. It can be seen as a consequence of concurrent events (such as the Paris terrorist attacks), as well as an attempt to earn some extra popular support in the last months before the Brexit vote. In its ideological dimension, Farage's discourse draws heavily upon isolationist voices in the proto-referendum debate, coming from opposition and the UK government alike. In general, the UKIP's Brexit discourse, addressing the popular feeling of anxiety and uncertainty about Britain's political and economic sovereignty, can be considered a precursor to many isolationist discourses in other countries of Europe and the EU.

5.1.2. Sovereignty and Pride in L&J's Discourse

The rhetoric of "national sovereignty" developed by Law & Justice in the 2015–19 parliamentary term reiterates many—if not most—of the themes occurring in the UKIP's Brexit discourse, particularly the central theme of migration and immigration policy in the EU. In the latter domain, rhetorical similarities of conceptual, pragmatic, and lexical nature are plentiful, notwithstanding some obvious differences in regard to geopolitical and historical context. The (anti-) immigration discourse of Law & Justice falls within a broader rhetorical and generally political stance, notoriously described in metaphoric terms as the politics of "rising from [the country's] knees" (in Polish "wstawać z kolan") and "not letting others pat you on the back" ("poklepywać po plecach"). This stance expresses, according to L&J supporters, the spirit of national pride and genuine sovereignty, that is a full independence from any foreign rule or influence (Leszczyński 2018). At the same time, it breaks with the arguably lenient attitude of the previous (Civic Platform) government.

In line with this orientation, L&J's (anti-)immigration discourse is a radically conservative, isolationist, and in many respects xenophobic kind of rhetoric, making use of explicitly coercive devices such as threat generation and fear appeals. In its thematic focus, it targets precisely the same domains as the UKIP and Nigel Farage's discourse, including national identity and sovereignty, economy, and welfare state, and, not least, state security and public safety. As will be shown, the main patterns of argument and the stylistic characterization are also largely similar, though one can observe in L&J's rhetoric some distinctive features of conceptual and text-structural nature, such as the conception of "alternative futures." We have noted in Chapter 3 (Section 3.3) that alternative futures, encompassing "privileged" and "oppositional" future types, are conceptual projections of alternative policy visions, which political speakers enact in virtual dialogues occurring in statements, comments, remarks, and other monologic forms. The main pragmatic function of alternative futures is the display of objective assessment and the performance of rationality and political legitimacy; thus, they come as handy conceptual ploys in discourses of policy legitimization such as (anti-)immigration discourse. In L&J's discourse, alternative futures permeate argument in all the thematic domains, from identity to security, being perhaps the most salient characteristic *not* originating from the UKIP's Brexit discourse.

Identity

Similar to Nigel Farage's rhetoric in the Brexit debate, national identity is a fundamental concept in L&J's discourse, providing necessary ideological foundations for the construction of argument rejecting the EU relocation schema. Identity-based argument serves to establish a firm and lasting *Us-vs.-Them* distinction, signaling issues and areas of possible political conflict (with the EU) as well as direct social clash (involving immigrants as such). The distinction is thus multidimensional; it subsumes a complex and heterogeneous *Them* category, which includes migrants construed as direct invader, but also EU institutions and their representatives as promoters of the relocation agenda. To draw up such a social, cultural, and political distinction, L&J leaders often appeal to the country's Christian heritage, from which they derive distinctive national values such as freedom, independence, tolerance, and, crucially, national pride. The latter is discursively related, less or more explicitly, to Polish historical legacy such as being at the heart of momentous developments in the history of Europe and the world (the Second World War, fall of communism, etc.). In that sense, L&J's rhetoric includes the idea of national exceptionalism, just like the UKIP's rhetoric. The concept of national legacy is used, in alternative future scenarios, as a precious commodity that must be safeguarded from any external danger or influence:

> (10) We are a proud, independent nation of free people whose character has been shaped in the most difficult and tragic moments of European history. We stand firm by our Christian heritage, the values to which our nation has been committed for centuries and to which we are committed today. As Christians, we are raised to be tolerant and respectful of other cultures. But we ask the same kind of respect from others. It is our right to decide whom we welcome to our own house. Because there are cultures, there are values, which simply cannot coexist. (PM Beata Szydło, September 5, 2016)

> (11) Our main responsibility is to uphold the well-being of Polish people. This has been our election promise and we will keep it. We will not trade our hard-won freedom and independence for political correctness. From the very beginning we have said that this issue [of immigration] should be resolved by assisting refugees outside the EU. We are staunchly against the European Commission proposal, which would force EU member states to pay millions of euros[7] per refused refugee. Such a decision would abolish the sovereignty of EU member states. We do not agree to that, we have to oppose that, because we are and we will be in charge in our own country. We do not take foreign orders. (Jarosław Kaczyński, September 5, 2016)

Made during a parliamentary debate on immigration, these two statements include the very essential identity claims in L&J's (anti-)immigration discourse. The main aim of these claims is to consolidate the home camp in its commitment to common values—such as freedom, independence, and tolerance—which stem from a common cultural and religious background. Such a consolidation is a prerequisite to reject alternative sociopolitical visions and projections, including the conception of multiculturalism and multicultural integration and, eventually, the admission of non-EU immigrants into Poland. At the heart of the rhetoric lies a strong appeal to the sense of "independence," which serves to invoke core elements of the national heritage in order to define and legitimize current and future responsibilities. The historical flashbacks in Szydło's speech (10) foster the spirit of exceptionalism, endorsing further claims of national uniqueness and implying particular rights that go with it, such as the "right to decide whom we welcome to our own house." The HOUSE metaphor, echoing the CONTAINER schema in the UKIP's Brexit discourse, adds to the aura of national solidarity invoked in both statements, cementing the social in-group and mobilizing it against possible negative scenarios, such as implementation of the EC proposal outlined in Kaczyński's statement (11). Notably, in addition to connoting positive values and triggering positive emotions, HOUSE can be conceptualized in terms of a "rupturable container" (Hart 2014), carrying presupposition of a possible damage, or destruction, from an external impact. The existence of such a presupposition is crucial to the argument in (10) and potentially also in (11), as the presupposed impact instills the aura of ideological as well as physical threat to the audience and the values addressed in both speeches. Kaczyński's speech includes a direct response to such threats, involving action following from a self-imposed obligation. As an "election promise" that the government "will keep" in the interest of its people, this obligation is essentially nonnegotiable and independent of any arising issues or circumstances. As such, it frees the government from abiding by other, external obligations, such as the relocation agreement.

The enactment of national identity in the statements by Szydło and Kaczyński is, as we noted, a prerequisite to have the audience reject scenarios construed as threatening to Polish cultural legacy and common values. This prerequisite is elaborated on in Kaczyński's speech (11), which makes use of the conceptual framework of alternative futures (Dunmire 2011; Cap 2021) to establish a direct contrast between two competing visions of the country's policy on immigration. One such vision, which can be described as Kaczyński's "oppositional future," involves following the EU relocation agenda approved by the former government. The other, his "privileged future," involves refusing to honor the agreement and the sanctions that protect it ("the European Commission proposal"). The distinction between the visions enacting the privileged and oppositional futures rests on the presence of specific lexical choices and structural configurations, and, with regard to the speaker's credibility and his persuasion effects, the presence of strategies activating specific uptake mechanisms. The linguistic, textual, and functional properties of the argument are, of course, mutually related. The oppositional future in (11) is construed through probabilistic modality ("would force," "would abolish") and draws on the use of items denoting largely abstract, underspecified concepts ("political correctness"). In contrast, the privileged future involves absolute modality expressed through categorical, unmediated assertions grounded in reality and addressing indisputable ideologies, truths, or commitments ("Our main responsibility is," "This has been our election promise and we will keep it," "We will not trade," and "We do not take foreign orders"). These truths and explicitly stated commitments constitute, along with rational assessment and direct solution proposals ("this issue should be resolved by"), the core evidential framework of the text. The salient presence of lexical material defining that framework is a crucial feature facilitating acceptance of ideational information (Halliday and Martin 1993; Gough and Talbot 1996). It thus adds to both easy comprehension and credibility of the speaker's message.

Regarding the latter properties, the distinction drawn in Kaczyński's text between the two alternative visions is strong enough to activate the principal mechanisms of successful uptake and persuasion, such as, most notably, the anti-thesis–thesis relation. According to rhetorical structure theory (RST) (Mann and Thompson 1988), the relation arises when two conceptions are contrasted, the speaker identifying with one and rejecting the other. From the RST perspective, an explicit contrast between two opposing positions expressed in a text sequence where the speaker's position is asserted as latter constitutes an argumentation device to enhance the speaker's ethos and endorse his choice as based upon rational consideration of options (Van Eemeren and Grootendorst 2004). Furthermore, the simplistic "black-and-white" nature of such a pattern facilitates a correct uptake of message communicated in the text. The argument in (11) involves an extremely explicit anti-thesis–thesis relation, which helps enact all of the aforementioned functions. Crucially, it makes the oppositional vision automatically and immediately rejectable, getting the audience favorably predisposed to the speaker's privileged vision. As a result, the argument unfolds according to Festinger's consistency principle (cf. Chapter 1, Section 1.3), providing the speaker with a substantial credibility credit prior to the enactment of his preferred vision. At the same time, the coherence markers used to set up the anti-thesis–thesis relation and the consistency sequence, such as cause-and-effect markers ("Such a decision would"), play their part in neutralizing the operation of logico-rhetorical deception modules in the speaker's audience (cf. 1.3).

Economy and Welfare State

Unlike identity claims in texts (10) and (11), issues of economy and welfare state are communicated mostly in speeches, statements, and comments that concentrate directly on migrants, pointing to "real reasons" behind mass immigration into Europe. In these statements, immigrants are often construed as cynical and selfish people, engaging in "benefit tourism" (Demetriou 2018) and thus abusing welfare systems in countries willing to accept them. Such a characterization establishes an explicit opposition between immigrant values and core Polish values, fueling ideologically based argument against the EU relocation schema. Integrating ideological and economic themes, this argument draws on the concept of morality in governance to define political norms to handle the immigration crisis. In many cases, such as Kaczyński's comment in (14), the argument goes well beyond ideological and welfare domains, including largely absurd anti-immigration claims involving quasi-scientific "knowledge." One can argue that the use of such (and other) claims defines L&J's discourse, in Norris and Inglehart's (2018) terms (cf. 3.4), as a true specimen of populist approach presupposing a great deal of ignorance in political audience:

> (12) We say no to those young healthy men who selfishly leave behind their wives and children to improve their own lives. We say no to those who choose to escape rather than fight for their country. (Beata Szydło, December 2, 2016)

> (13) Some have suggested creating barriers to prevent immigration is immoral. Then why do people build walls, fences, and gates around their homes? They don't build walls because they hate the people on the outside but because they love their families on the inside. The only thing that is immoral is the politicians to do nothing and continue to allow hard-working Europeans to be so horribly exploited. (Witold Waszczykowski, April 23, 2016)

> (14) Have we forgotten that, in the past, migrants brought diseases like cholera and dysentery to Europe, as well as all sorts of parasites and protozoa, which while not dangerous in the organisms of these people, could be dangerous here. (Jarosław Kaczyński, December 19, 2015)

Once again, examples (12–14) come from parliamentary sessions devoted to immigration and the EU relocation agenda. Overall, they conceptualize immigrants as unpatriotic, greedy, and guided by their individual economic interest (12). Such a construal draws a sharp distinction between immigrant values and Polish, as well as generally European, values. Thus, in (13) argument is made in the name of those countries that allowed non-European immigrants to settle. The presumption of moral right to speak on behalf of others in Waszczykowski's statement is not a new motif; it clearly inscribes into historical narration of Poland's conservative groups in the Third Republic (cf. Chapter 2). Within this narration, Poland is viewed as a unique country, the "Messiah of nations" and "a defender of the Catholic faith in Europe" (Gomola 2019). This perception follows from the country's martyrdom in the past, but also, more recently, from the influence of Pope John Paul II and, not least, from Solidarity's historical victory over the communist government in the 1989 elections. As argued by Polish conservatives, all these facts and factors make Poland particularly entitled to an assertive presence in Europe. Such a position is indeed salient in Waszczykowski's argument (13), which aims to define moral standards and political norms to deal with the migration crisis. Finally, Kaczyński's comment in (14) can be described as the most direct manifestation of L&J's xenophobic stance, laying the foundations for further threat-based discourse concerning state security and public safety. From a conceptual and structural standpoint, both his remark and Waszczykowski's statement convey their messages—just like the earlier texts—within the framework of alternative futures. Oppositional future involves, in both speeches, a vaguely defined projection supported by probabilistic modality and mediated evidential claims ("Some have suggested," "Have we forgotten," "could be dangerous," etc.). In contrast, privileged future subsumes, in Waszczykowski's text, absolute modality ("The only thing that is immoral is") and factual evidence ("people build walls, fences. . ."). Notably, privileged future in Kaczyński's text is not marked explicitly, but emerges as a presumed answer to the rhetorical question opening the comment.

Public Safety

Issues of state security and public safety play a key role in L&J's argument against the EU relocation schema. Developing the vision of immigration as a tangible, potentially physical threat, L&J's discourse makes salient the *Us*-vs.-

Them distinctions drawn previously in other domains, such as the domain of cultural and religious identity. These distinctions and differences are now presented as irreconcilable and eventually threatening. As a rule, the security discourse of Law & Justice reveals some precisely structured argumentation patterns, involving fixed lexical, grammatical, and text organization choices. The most frequent of these patterns are alternative future scenarios and, notably, the interplay of axiological and spatial/physical meanings in the process of discursive proximization. As we have seen earlier in the book, such an interplay is characterized by a sequential structure of argument whereby axiological proximization is introduced first to establish an abstract distant vision and spatiotemporal proximization is used subsequently to redefine that vision in terms of a material threat. The mechanism in question is exemplified in the following text (15). Example (16) shows, in turn, how L&J's security argument exploits the pragmatic powers of alternative future scenarios. Both examples come from parliamentary sessions devoted to discussion of the EU relocation schema:

> **(15)** Our position has been clear from the beginning. The issue of immigration from the Middle East should be resolved where it has originated. By advancing freedom and democracy in Syria and Iraq, we help end a cycle of <u>dictatorship and radicalism</u>$_{NP}$ that <u>brings millions of people to misery and frustration</u>$_{VP}$, and <u>brings danger and, one day, tragedy to</u>$_{VP}$ <u>our own people</u>$_{NP}$. (Jarosław Kaczyński, May 13, 2016)

> **(16)** Do we want to have districts where sharia law reigns? Where there are no-go zones for police. And where every few weeks something explodes. We could let them [immigrants] in, wait and hope that they integrate. This is precisely what Brussels and Stockholm have tried. And this is also what Nice has tried.[8] Here in Poland, our predecessors[9] were on track to commit the same mistakes as other Western countries. But the new government sets the priorities right. This government knows that the safety of Polish citizens comes first. (Mariusz Błaszczak, July 17, 2016)

In example (15) Jarosław Kaczyński sets up an explicit link between the social and political conditions of immigrants' lives in their home countries ("Syria and Iraq"), and their social and psychological effects ("misery and frustration"), which can trigger disastrous consequences in the long run, once immigrants arrive in Poland ("one day, tragedy, to our own people"). Such a logic is meant to support L&J's rationale for handling the immigration issue far away from European borders. Kaczyński's argument unfolds in a linear manner, connecting apparently remote visions with, eventually, closely happening events. At the lexical level, nominal phrases are used to mark the *Us*-vs.-*Them* opposition in ideological terms ("our people" vs. people living in "dictatorship and radicalism"), and verbal phrases ("brings millions of people," "brings danger") are applied to proximize *Them*'s anticipated impact. Generally, the argument involves a discursive transition from a starting scenario of "remote possibility" to a redefined scenario of "actual occurrence." Each of the scenarios is enacted linguistically by the combination of a nominal phrase (NP) with a verb phrase (VP)—as indicated by the subscript in (15). The interplay of axiological and spatiotemporal proximizations underlying the scenarios can be represented as follows (Figure 5.1).

In (16), the argument develops around conceptualizations of alternative futures. Interior Minister Mariusz Błaszczak outlines an oppositional future that involves dormant presence of material threats to public safety, particularly a looming terrorist threat. This vision derives its credibility from ideological and cultural premises that have been tested and endorsed in L&J's

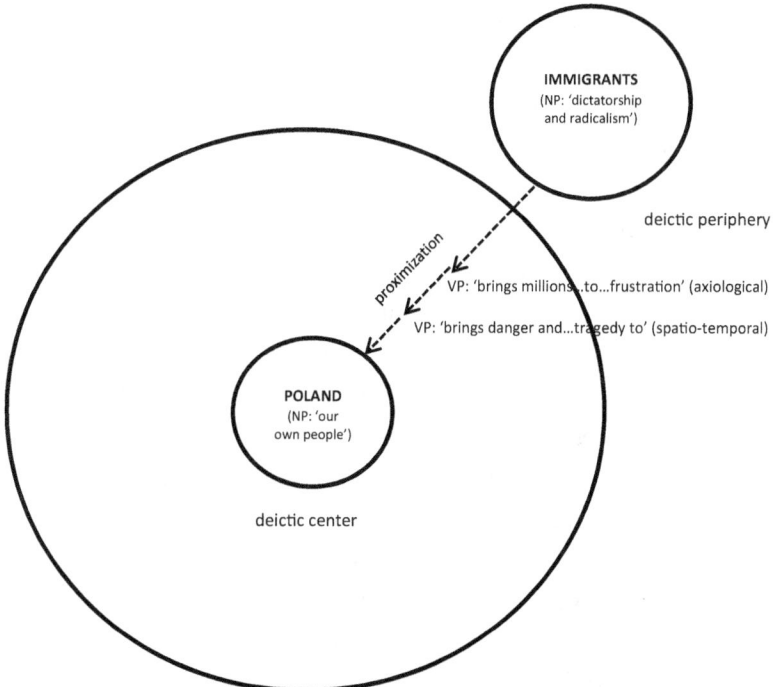

Figure 5.1 Axiological and spatiotemporal proximization in (15).

argument on immigration in other domains (such as identity, economy, and welfare state) and can now be taken for granted. Specifically, the massive number of migrants from Africa and the Middle East and their inability to integrate in Europe (likely resulting in frustration and anger) are construed as a potential source of threat to local communities in European cities. This premise is further validated by a flashback example of a terrorist attack in Nice perpetrated by an Islamic immigrant. The mention of the Nice attack is, incidentally, a close copy of Nigel Farage's argument made at BBC station on the same day, July 17 (see example 8). The oppositional vision in Błaszczak's speech includes, additionally, the absence of resources to handle the threat ("no-go zones for police," "districts where sharia law reigns"), resulting—as can be inferred—from EU's excessively multiculturalist stance and ultra-liberal immigration policies. The enactment of the oppositional vision in the text involves standard lexico-grammatical choices, such as interrogative mood ("Do we want"), probabilistic modality ("could let them in"), and evidential phrases expressing passivity and mental speculation ("wait and hope").

The oppositional future in Błaszczak's speech is deftly followed by privileged future, which is a future based on rational judgment, learning from past experience ("This is . . . what Brussels and Stockholm have tried. And this is also what Nice has tried") and, crucially, consistently following the ideological principles and values delineated in anti-immigration arguments in other domains (examples 10–14). According to these principles, "the safety of Polish citizens comes first," which constitutes an irrefutable premise detracting from an external obligation to follow the EU relocation plan. The privileged future is thus not only a future of rational, "patriotic" decisions on the international arena but also of a new kind of governance in general. This extra element of legitimization of L&J's political leadership is well visible in the speech ("our predecessors were on track to commit the same mistakes . . . But the new government sets the priorities right"). Linguistically, the performance of privileged future in Błaszczak's text involves the use of declarative mood, absolute modality, and categorical, unmediated assertions expressing certainty, rather than belief ("knows," "sets . . . right"). The triggers of rhetorical uptake, which we identified before (cf. 10–11), are continually salient: the anti-thesis–thesis sequential relation and deictic markers of coherence remain in place to enhance credibility and persuasion effects.

The argument in (16) can be described as the ultimate proof of a close relation, in regard to migration issues, between UKIP's rhetoric in the Brexit campaign and the discourse used by L&J leaders to further the image of Poland as a "proud and sovereign nation state" that rejects any "centrally imposed dictate," as Kaczyński once called the EU relocation agenda.[10] As has been shown, similarities between the two discourses can be found at several levels: conceptual, pragmatic, as well as linguistic, that is lexical, text-structural, and grammatical. At the conceptual level, both enact a strongly exceptionalist stance, building their argument upon ideological premises. The argument focuses, in both cases, on issues of identity, economy, and public safety. As a rule, the credibility earned through identity-related claims serves to endorse further claims in the other domains, particularly in the area of state security and public safety. At the pragmatic and pragmalinguistic levels, both discourses make ample use of the coercive strategy of proximization, though in L&J's discourse proximization is used, apparently, in a more structured way, involving recurrent presence of spatio-axiological semantic patterns. At the same time, UKIP's discourse makes a frequent use of other strategies drawing upon spatial awareness and cognition, such as metaphorization (especially the STATE IS CONTAINER metaphor). This can, of course, be attributed to geopolitical as well as plainly geographical context, that is, the island location of the UK. In L&J's rhetoric, metaphorization is employed to establish cultural and religious, rather than geopolitical, distinctions. Also, L&J's discourse seems quite unique in outlining political visions through "alternative futures," a strategy that occurs rarely in Nigel Farage's speeches. Finally, at the linguistic level, both discourses demonstrate a number of recurrent structural and lexico-grammatical units and patterns, such as anti-thesis–thesis relations and consistency sequences.

The existence of all these similarities and analogies goes to illustrate how influential the UKIP's Brexit rhetoric has been in providing resources to shape Eurosceptic attitudes in people not just inside but also outside the UK. While the "success" of the UKIP's Eurosceptic discourse in Britain has already been verified in the 2016 Brexit referendum, the political effects of "sovereignty discourse" of Law & Justice are yet to be seen. It is telling, however, to compare the rates of approval of Poland's membership in the EU in the last few years. Consecutive Eurobarometer surveys[11] show that while in April 2015 the support of Poles for the country's membership in the EU hit a record high of

91 percent, it dropped to 85 percent two years later, and then to 77 percent in 2019, at the end of L&J's first parliamentary term. As this book is being written, the approval rate is even lower, at 74 percent (as of September 2020). A "Polexit" may still look distant, but trendlines are clear. They become even clearer if we consider that Eurosceptic voices are heard from L&J not only in regard to migration issues—they become increasingly louder in other, critical domains.

5.2. Defending the Judicial Reform

In the rich history of crises and conflicts between Warsaw and Brussels that arose after 2015, the conflict over L&J's reform of the Polish judiciary appears as the most consequential and, arguably, the most threatening to Poland's future membership in the EU. We have observed in the previous chapter that the sweeping changes introduced by Law & Justice in the judicial sector, involving its cornerstone institutions such as the Constitutional Tribunal and the Supreme Court, were deemed unconstitutional by the European Commission, which found several new provisions contrary to EU law. A sizable list of recommendations for amendments were issued subsequently, but these were blatantly disregarded by the L&J government. As a result, in November 2017 the European Parliament triggered in relation to Poland Article 7 of the Treaty on European Union. As we noted before (cf. 4.2.1), the Article involves a procedure under which membership rights of a state can be suspended, as punishment for breaching EU's founding values, which include, among others, a consistent commitment to the rule of law. The EP resolution regarding application of Article 7 was passed by a vast majority of votes, which included also the votes of fourteen Polish MEPs, most of whom were former members of the Civic Platform party.

The passing of the resolution can be regarded as a critical moment in the evolution of L&J's sovereignty discourse. Indeed, the years 2018–19 see an unprecedented number of speeches, statements, and comments in which Kaczyński, Morawiecki, and other L&J leaders use the concepts of independence and national sovereignty as viable rhetorical instruments to defend the ongoing reform of the judiciary and present the consecutive changes as legitimate. Realizing this goal involves a simultaneous use of two strategies of communication, internal and external. On the one hand, L&J's discourse targets home opponents of the reform, describing them as unpatriotic and serving foreign interests. We have noted the most extreme cases of such an argument in the previous chapter. On the other hand, L&J reacts to the application of Article 7 (and other manifestations of EU's position) in its international discourse, by criticizing and often openly attacking EU institutions, countries, and even individual EU politicians for their alleged encroachment on Poland's rights as a free and independent state. Needless to say, both strategies are meant to make a common contribution to the ruling party's approval rates at home.

The most comprehensive international articulation of L&J's reaction to the implementation of Article 7 is, without doubt, the document meant as a formal response to the EP resolution, titled "White Paper on the Reform of the Polish Judiciary" (henceforth referred to as "the Paper"). Signed by Prime Minister Morawiecki, it was delivered to Brussels on March 7, 2018, while simultaneously being published on the official website of Poland's government (http://www.premier.gov.pl). The publication of the Paper was broadly communicated in the Polish media, many of which (particularly those favorably disposed toward the ruling party) encouraged people to read the government's response. That way, the Paper became widely known among politicians, journalists, and ordinary people alike, inspiring a number of follow-up statements and comments. The main lines of argument underlying the Paper can be readily identified from its introductory passages, including, among others, general remarks on the status and functioning of the European Union:

> **(17)** The EU must be built on a foundation of law and legal certainty. Without this principle, the European Union will only be a mechanism for making arbitrary decisions by Eurocrats, and de facto by the European oligarchy. We say an explicit "yes" to the EU, but an explicit "no" to the mechanisms that rebuke us—like children—and treat Poland and other EU countries unequally. From the economic point of view, the European Union is a group of states that are bound by bilateral dependencies. The EU derives many benefits from Poland's membership. Around 2 million Poles have left our country and work for our partners in the EU. Another benefit is, for example, the free movement of capital. It is not right that we have French shops, Dutch companies and German media, and Poland's government is

denied the right to introduce its own sovereign institutional solutions, such as judicial reforms to which we are entitled pursuant to the European Treaty. We want the EU to be a fair mechanism. It is a Polish and EU reason of state to ensure that European principles of equality are respected. The European Union is great when it is a Europe of Homelands and when it can cooperate. It must respect diversity concerning not only economy, but also system of justice. Therefore, we are fighting for Poland and for the future of the EU at the same time. (White Paper on the Reform of the Polish Judiciary, March 7, 2018, https://www.premier.gov.pl/files/files/white_paper_en_full.pdf)

While the official title of the Paper implies its focus on predominantly legal matters, we can see from this excerpt that the actual scope of the document is much broader, involving issues of economy and governance, as well as foundational questions of the political status of the EU. The particular themes and their domains are often interrelated or follow one another closely, creating ad hoc conflations of concepts and ideas that are normally conceptually incongruent or just thematically different, such as "free movement of capital" and "system of justice." Some of these ideas are developed in striking detail; the text in (17) includes, for instance, a mention of "2 million Poles" working abroad and an illustration of the impact of French, Dutch, and German capital in Poland. At the same time, some ideas are not developed, especially regarding their contribution to the main argument in the Paper. This can be said, for example, about the "Europe of Homelands," a concept that is left unelaborated and unexplained. Altogether, the text demonstrates thematic and structural inconsistencies, which could lead to its being deemed unworthy of analytic attention. This, however, could be a fallacious move, and particularly so given the target audience of the Paper. As has been noted, the document was designed for multiple audiences—formally for Brussels officials, but in fact also for a vast number of other political and social groups, including, not least, "ordinary Poles."

With this in mind, one can regard a number of structural and semantic ploys in the text as strategic. First of all, the very condensation of different topics, concepts, and ideas in the text detracts from an issue that authors are apparently reluctant to discuss, that is, the condition of the rule of law in Poland. In bringing up alternative themes, the Paper performs what political commentators often refer to as a "forward escape" strategy: dodging the principal issue by offering numerous—always eye-catching—"distractors" (Billig 1996). In this case, the distractors are issues that attract in themselves large public attention and often trigger controversy, such as division of competency between the EU and member states. The characterization of the European Union in broad sociopolitical and economic terms as "a group of states that are bound by bilateral dependencies" and the argument that follows can thus be seen as a premeditated digression from the principal legal theme. The same can be said of other comments on the functioning of the EU in its present form, especially the criticism of Brussels' arbitrariness in decision-making.

It can be easily noticed that the Paper often refers to legal and economic issues at the same time, most conspicuously in the sentence: "it [the EU] must respect diversity concerning not only economy but also system of justice." This regularity can also be considered a conceptual and pragmatic strategy. It consists in conflation of a straightforward and essentially indisputable idea with a concept that invites multiple and often different interpretations. As the ideas of business and economic diversity and free flow of goods evoke predominantly positive connotations within the economic domain, they are used as a premise to argue for analogical arrangements within another, legal domain. The problem is that the concept of "diversity" in European and particularly EU law is far more complex, and entails several interpretations, which are precisely defined and codified in EU founding documents. Many of these codifications are in fact contrary to L&J's concept of the Union as such. This includes, notably, primacy of EU law over national law (Kwiecień 2006) in relation to specific legal areas and proceedings, such as interpretation of laws included in the national constitution. However, the Paper aims to conceal these interpretations, by highlighting positive aspects of "diversity," which it "borrows," in a sense, from the economic domain. As a result, it presents L&J's aspirations as fully legitimate and essentially in line with EU's geopolitical mission. Furthermore, it construes the L&J government as a staunch supporter and defender of this mission, as in "we are fighting for Poland and for the future of the EU at the same time."

In its designation for Polish audience, the Paper fits in with several of the inherent sociopsychological predispositions of Polish people. Most crucially, it addresses a firm sense of historical injustice, shaped over centuries of subordination to political giants such as Russia and Germany (see Chapter 2). Invoking the metaphoric concept of state as a person, and focusing on attributes of maturity and immaturity, it construes the EU stance toward Poland in further metaphoric terms of usurped "parenthood." Thus, it considers any "mechanisms that rebuke us [Poland]—like children" as essentially illegitimate, deriving from overblown ambitions and aspirations of "Eurocrats." It also implies, at its deepest level, threats of political and economic subordination to Brussels that recall the darkest periods of Poland's political dependence, such as the communist era. Doing so, it echoes—however implicitly—one of the most favorite catchphrases of Polish nationalist groups, namely, "wczoraj Moskwa, dziś Bruksela" ["yesterday (it was) Moscow, today (it is) Brussels"]. Incidentally, since Article 7 was triggered, the frequency of this phrase has been on the rise among L&J politicians as well.

Speaking of these similarities and analogies, the argument in the Paper is indeed widely reiterated in L&J's spoken discourse, especially in 2018. Such follow-up statements are invariably more explicit, not to say blatant (Sofizade 2019). The following examples come from one of 2018 European Parliament debates on the situation of rule of law in Poland. The debate took place on March 14, a week after the L&J government sent the Paper to Brussels:

(18) Poland is a proud country, please don't lecture us on such matters. We are perfectly aware of how to manage our institutions. (MEP Beata Kempa, March 14, 2018)

(19) You have never lived under communism, have you? You don't understand us, you don't understand Polish politics, you are looking at it through the lens of your own political reality. (MEP Beata Szydło, March 14, 2018)

(20) In this chamber this is not about dialogue, this isn't debate, let's not pull the wool over our eyes, this is again a show of force addressed to the Poles and the Polish government. This isn't about the rule of law, it's about raw power and who possesses it. (MEP Patryk Jaki, March 14, 2018)

(21) I remember there were times when Soviet diplomats declared their willingness to help in their satellite countries. These are colonial habits, you know, Eastern Europe is suddenly ready to act, to do something, to be independent. And I think it's time the rest of you understood that Eastern Europe has now found its way, and it's not going to ask permission each time. (MEP Ryszard Legutko, March 14, 2018)

The statements in (18–21) come from Polish MEPs who were formerly L&J MPs in Poland. They develop and strengthen most of the points included in the Paper, particularly Brussels' alleged aspirations for political control over Poland, and in fact also over other countries of the former Soviet bloc. The tone of these remarks is as harsh as it is accusatory, describing EU practices as "colonial" (21) and essentially anti-Polish (20: "a show of force addressed to the Poles and the Polish government"). The statements in (18) and (19) emphasize historical and geopolitical ignorance of "old members" of the EU, which apparently "do not understand" Poland, its "political reality" and, crucially, the deep and lasting impact of communism on its institutions, including the legal system. This argument is highly representative of L&J's narration concerning the EU-contested legal reform. The essence of the argument is that Poland, unlike most Western countries, is entitled to extraordinary measures in reforming its judiciary. This is, arguably, because Poland's judicial sector remains under the influence of former (communist) elites and thus cannot function as a guarantor of justice in the new democratic state (Sofizade 2019). The presumption of historical ignorance on the part of the EU occurs, incidentally, in other domains as well. One such domain is economic relations, specifically the threat of exclusion of economically weaker countries (such as Poland) as a result of business agreements between European hegemons. According to L&J, EU position toward such threats is negligent and passive, despite painful lessons of the past. We look at this issue in the final chapter.

6

Oppressed by Neighbors
Germany, Russia, and Nord Stream 2

We have seen from our discussion so far that L&J's politics of reliance on threat generation and crisis management to obtain policy legitimization simultaneously follows and departs from broader sociopolitical and rhetorical trends in the contemporary Europe. Rather than playing on the existing political, social, and ideological divisions, L&J's practice is to use discourse that itself generates and perpetuates the aura of conflict across multiple domains, both home and abroad. The aim is to exploit the arising tensions and crises as a coercive premise for the enactment of strong political leadership. In this final chapter we move to the domain of economy, focusing on the relations between Poland and its two powerful neighbors: Germany and Russia. Specifically, we explore L&J's discourse opposing the Nord Stream 2 (NS2) project, that is, construction of a gas pipeline enabling direct export of gas from Russia to Germany bypassing traditional transit countries, such as Poland, Ukraine, Belarus, Slovakia, and the Czech Republic. The data include statements by L&J MPs made at parliamentary sessions (including EP sessions), as well as official communications of the Polish government. They come mostly from the years 2018–19—the period of highest tensions and controversies surrounding the NS2 project so far.

The chapter shows how NS2 is discursively construed by the L&J government as a gathering threat to the development of Poland's economy and, potentially, Poland's national security. It describes lexical, conceptual, and pragmatic tools that are used to present NS2 in terms of a revival of imperialistic ambitions of European hegemons, a mindset that is historically responsible for devastating political projects, including the infamous 1939 Nazi–Soviet Molotov-

Ribbentrop Pact. It explains the conceptual operations and mechanisms underlying L&J's NS2 rhetoric, whose function is to impose construals of geopolitical isolation and economic exclusion of Poland. As is demonstrated, such construals draw on specific metaphoric schemas, most typically the STATE IS PERSON metaphor. In their coercive and fear-inducing appeal, they rely on conceptual strategies of proximization, such as spatially perceived visions of external influence and impact. The chapter shows how these threatening visions contribute to the mobilization and consolidation of L&J's electorate in Poland, ensuring its unfaltering support for L&J's leadership. At the same time, it points to the criticism of the NS2 project in other Central and Eastern European countries, including Ukraine and the Czech Republic. It is observed that none of the anti-NS2 voices in these countries comes anywhere close to L&J's discourse in terms of its inherent coercive properties and legitimization goals.

6.1. NS2: An Energy Wonder or a New Molotov-Ribbentrop Pact?

What exactly is Nord Stream 2 (NS2)? We need a precise picture of the project to understand its many economic, social, political, and eventually discursive implications. NS2 is an underwater twin pipeline that would transport natural gas from Russia directly to Germany. At a length of 1,230 kilometers, it is to follow the route of the existing Nord Stream twin pipeline underneath the Baltic Sea. The original Nord Stream pipeline, with an annual capacity of 55 billion cubic meters, was finished in late 2012. The pipeline system's total capacity is set to double to 110 billion cubic meters following Nord Stream 2's completion. The pipeline crosses into the exclusive economic zones of five countries: Russia, Germany, Denmark, Finland, and Sweden. Moscow-based, state-owned Gazprom company is the project's sole shareholder providing 50 percent of the project's financing, with the remaining funds coming from German, Dutch, French, and Austrian oil and gas companies. The total cost of the project is estimated at around 9.5 billion euros.

The project's supporters, which include the Russian government, the companies involved, most EU leaders, and a vast majority of German politicians, argue that the pipeline would both increase security of gas supply by connecting

Western Europe to the world's biggest gas reserves and support European sustainability goals by replacing coal as a less CO_2-intensive complement to renewable energies. For instance, Germany is planning on phasing out its coal use in order to meets its CO_2 emissions reduction targets, which will further strain its electricity grid. Supporters of the project in Germany also argue that Nord Stream 2 could provide the energy currently supplied by nuclear power plants, which are planned to be taken offline by 2022. In a 2017 study, energy research and consultancy organization ewi Energy Research & Scenarios wrote that Nord Stream 2 would also help bring down gas prices in the EU. "When Nord Stream 2 is available, Russia can supply more gas to the EU, decreasing the need to import more expensive LNG.[1] Hence, the import price for the remaining LNG volumes decreases, thereby reducing the overall EU-28[2] price level," wrote ewi (cf. the study at https://www.ewi.research-scenarios.de/cms/wp-content/uploads/2017/09/EWI-1163-17-Studie-Impacts-of-Nord-Stream-2-web.compressed.pdf).

EU's own position on NS2, which can be described as generally (though not unequivocally) approving, stresses the fact that Russian gas reserves are among the most cost-effective sources from which to supply Europe. At the same time, they are available and deliverable at short notice. This makes Russian piped gas, despite objections of political nature, the best option for EU's gas supply. As noted by Sziklai, Koczy, and Csercsik (2019), EU clearly recognizes the fact that with global demand rising over 25 percent until 2035 and its own gas resources depleting, it needs to secure gas resources in the long term in order to ensure global industrial competitiveness. EU industry in particular needs reasonably priced energy if it is not to relocate production to other world regions. Thus, compared with other suppliers and transport options (such as the LNG), Nord Stream 2 is considered, in economic terms, the most competitive supply source.

The argument against NS2 is equally widespread, including clearly adversarial positions of the United States and countries of Central and Eastern Europe, as well as skeptical opinions of several EU and German politicians and, not least, a number of environmental groups. It is claimed that the pipeline would harm fragile marine ecosystems, jeopardize the move of the EU bloc to a low-carbon economy, increase European reliance on Russia for energy to a dangerous level, and empower Russia at a time that it is facing criticism for destabilizing activities around the globe (Sziklai, Koczy, and Csercsik 2019).

Each of these arguments is taken further within its original domain. From the economic perspective, projections for future EU gas demand very widely, with some calling into question the need for extra import capacities. In a 2018 paper, the German Institute for Economic Research (DIW) writes that the energy consumption forecasts on which Nord Stream 2 is based "significantly overestimate natural gas demand in Germany and Europe" and that there will be no supply gap if the pipeline is not built (see the full paper at http://www.cleanenergywire.org/experts/diw-german-institute-economic-research). At the same time, some climate change activists maintain that even if natural gas were friendlier to the climate than coal, the project should be abandoned. In their view, the combustion of natural gas contributes to global warming, and the construction of the NS2 pipeline represents an investment that will "lock" Germany—and the EU—into fossil fuels "for decades" (Bouwmeester and Oosterhaven 2017: 68). Marine conservation groups also oppose the project, arguing that laying new pipelines under the Baltic Sea would lead to highly detrimental effects on ecosystems. The German Nature and Biodiversity Conservation Union had tried unsuccessfully to halt construction before local courts and the Federal Constitutional Court (Sziklai, Koczy, and Csercsik 2019).

International security issues are, of course, of particular importance to political context of NS2 and its effects on discourse. Here, the most powerful opponent of the project has been the United States. The administrations of both Presidents Barack Obama and Donald Trump have expressed their opposition to the pipeline, and the country introduced sanctions in December 2018, forcing pipelaying vessels by a Swiss company to stop working on the project and leading to a months-long delay. The American government contends that completion of the project would increase European reliance on Russia and imperil the continent's security policy at a time when Russia is facing intense criticism for its alleged interference in Western democracies, aggression in Eastern Europe, and support of Syrian President Bashar al-Assad. In view of this, Donald Trump's Secretary of State Mike Pompeo called Nord Stream 2 one of "Russia's malign influence projects" (Bouwmeester and Oosterhaven 2017: 71). The American argument rests on the premise that because Gazprom is a state-owned enterprise, purchasing gas from the company funnels money directly to the government that is then used to commit nefarious activities both domestically and around the world.

In Pompeo's words, "money from gas and oil exports allow today's leaders in Moscow to do what they like doing most: enrich themselves; halt reforms; and grow the military, the FSB[3] and the police apparatus" (Bouwmeester and Oosterhaven 2017: 72).

Finally, let alone Poland, many other countries of Central and Eastern Europe, such as Slovakia, the Czech Republic, and Ukraine, oppose Nord Stream 2, partially because of their expectations of a loss of transit fees and partially because of fears that their economic and eventually physical security would be jeopardized were the project to be completed. Speaking at a 2018 plenary session of the European Parliament, the Czech Prime Minister Andrej Babiš observes:

> **(1)** Nord Stream 2 neither aligns with the energy and foreign policy interests of many of EU member states nor complies with the bloc's long-term strategy to achieve an Energy Union. As a matter of fact, Nord Stream 2 could impede the development of an open gas market with price competition and diversified supply to the EU. Even worse, it could reshape the security architecture of Europe, making it more vulnerable. It could be used to separate markets and exercise market power in Central and Eastern Europe, Southeastern Europe, and even Italy. (PM Andrej Babiš, February 13, 2018)

Babiš's words paint a representative picture of long-existent objections to the NS2 project, involving economic as well as security aspects. However, it can be noticed that, as the project progresses, strong objections of political nature become particularly salient. A recent TV statement by the president of Ukraine, Volodymyr Zelensky, is an example:

> **(2)** Nord Stream 2 is a tool Russia is using to support its continued aggression against Ukraine. Russia seeks to prevent it from integrating more closely with Europe and the United States. Nord Stream 2 would enable Russia to bypass Ukraine for gas transit to Europe, which would deprive Ukraine of substantial transit revenues and increase its vulnerability to Russian aggression. Nord Stream 2 would also help maintain Europe's significant reliance on imports of Russian natural gas, which creates economic and political vulnerabilities for our EU partners and their allies. For these reasons, the government of Ukraine will continue to oppose Nord Stream 2. (President Volodymyr Zelensky for 24/7 News TV channel in Kiev, June 6, 2019)

The growing focus on security issues is accompanied, especially in Central European countries, by the perception of Germany and Russia as only participants in the NS2 project. In the words of Slovak Prime Minister Peter Pellegrini,[4]

> **(3)** it's very sad when Germany makes a massive oil and gas deal with Russia, where you're supposed to be guarding against Russia and Germany goes out and pays billions and billions of dollars a year to Russia. (PM Peter Pellegrini at the Bratislava meeting of the Visegrád Group, December 2, 2018[5])

Notably, in Pellegrini's statement, the words "Russia" and "Germany" appear, next to each other, five times within the space of a single sentence. At the same time, there is no mention of other key players, such as the EU and the countries whose companies are involved in the construction process. This kind of argument has a specific rhetorical function: it invokes the vision of an elitist deal that is supposed to benefit the few, at the likely expense of the many. Pellegrini's remark furthers this vision by making explicit the financial side of the deal, involving billion-dollar transactions between the two countries.

Altogether, the many different contexts of NS2, and its urgent political and security implications in particular, lay the fertile ground for coercive, threat-based discourse. This is clearly reflected in policy legitimization discourse of the Polish government, especially during the last months of the 2015–19 parliamentary term. The threatening visions salient in L&J's discourse of NS2 construe the project as an element of economic and political oppression, exerted on Poland by European hegemons. The latter include Poland's giant neighbors, Russia and Germany, but—indirectly—also the main EU players and EU governing institutions as such. In that sense, a significant part of discourse on NS2 inscribes in L&J's generally Eurosceptic stance manifested in regard to other social and institutional issues. In fact, as we see herein, in attacking the project L&J politicians never skip opportunity to address these issues if they consider such digressions politically beneficial:

> **(4)** The NS2 project is a clear and growing threat. The Russian ambassador to Belarus suggested last week when the Baltic pipeline is built, Gazprom would be able to cut off Belarus and Poland without cutting off Germany. Poland has a particular sensitivity to corridors and deals above our head. That was the Locarno tradition,[6] that was the Molotov-Ribbentrop tradition.

That was the 20th century. We don't want any repetition of that. (Jarosław Kaczyński for TVP1 public television channel, April 5, 2019)

(5) Speaking as Prime Minister of Poland, I must say it is unwise for the European Commission to try to play deaf, dumb and blind to certain serious developments in the real world. It is unwise to pretend that things are normal in the EU-Russia energy business. The fact is that Russia's gas pipelines, the little green men that it sent to Ukraine, and its anti-EU propaganda are all part of the same program. The European Commission is so worried about rule of law in Poland. Instead of interfering with Poland's rights as a sovereign state, I would like to hear Commission president Jean-Claude Juncker take a clear stand on NS2. I myself call it a killer project because I believe it is part of a program to destroy European unity. (PM Mateusz Morawiecki at the European Parliament, April 16, 2019)

(6) NS2 is a killer project because it shows that Schroederism is back in Europe. I am talking about the former German chancellor, Gerhard Schroeder's policy of putting Russian money first. It risks making Germany, one of the most powerful EU states, prone to Russian manipulation. You hear Schroederism from people in chancellor Angela Merkel's cabinet. You sometimes hear it from the chancellor herself. Angela Merkel recently spoke out in defense of EU energy security, but she also defended the commercial merit of NS2. (PM Mateusz Morawiecki at the European Parliament, April 16, 2019)

Looking at these examples, a majority of conceptual, pragmatic, and lexical ploys, which we discussed in previous chapters, are there. Crucially, in the text of Kaczyński's interview (example 4) the NS2 project is defined as "a clear and growing threat," which represents a strategy of proximization that is realized through the use of progressive aspect and lexical nominalization detracting from temporal specificity of the threat element. As has been noted, this kind of construal adds to the envisaged caliber of the threat. The scenario outlined in the first two sentences of (4) can be described in conceptual terms as the speaker's "oppositional future," deriving from mediated evidence ("Russian ambassador to Belarus suggested") and expressed through probabilistic modality ("would be able to cut off"). Such an ominous vision is countered, at the end of the text, with a strong enactment of "privileged future," a reassuring vision of political control over the situation. The positive vision earns its credibility from the apparent rationality and historical awareness of Kaczyński and his party colleagues as political leaders. The latter traits are meant to emerge from two historical analogies—"traditions"—which are strategically invoked to underscore the commitment and competence of L&J politicians.

Of these two flashbacks, the mention of "the Molotov-Ribbentrop [Pact]" is particularly forceful and potentially the most effective in rhetorical and legitimization terms. The Molotov-Ribbentrop Pact was a nonaggression pact between Nazi Germany and the Soviet Union that enabled those two powers to partition Poland between them. Its clauses provided a guarantee of peace by each party toward the other and a commitment that declared that neither government would ally itself to or aid an enemy of the other. In addition to the publicly announced stipulations of nonaggression, the Pact included a secret protocol that defined the borders of Soviet and German spheres of influence across Poland (Hehn 2005). As such, the Molotov-Ribbentrop Pact has come to symbolize one of the most brutal and cynical backroom deals of world superpowers against Poland in history. Using it as an analogy to the NS2 initiative, Kaczyński assumes an essentially antagonistic tone that applies later to virtually all other instances of L&J's discourse concerning the project. This can be readily seen from examples (5) and (6), containing excerpts of PM Morawiecki's address to the European Parliament in April 2019. Taking place less than two weeks after Kaczyński's interview, the speech by Morawiecki is in many ways a follow-up performance of explicitly adversarial stance toward NS2 and the key players in the project.

Interestingly, Morawiecki's argument seems designed mostly for the home audience. This can be seen from the reference, in (5), to the "rule of law in Poland" and "Poland's rights as a sovereign state." By criticizing the European Commission's slow response to threats allegedly posed by the NS2 project ("I would like to hear . . . Jean-Claude Juncker take a clear stand on NS2"), Morawiecki aims to contest EU's mandate to act internationally on other matters, such as assessment of judicial reforms in member states. In this way, critique of NS2 becomes an element in the overall pattern of policy legitimization sought by the L&J government. At the same time, the concept of national sovereignty resurfaces within not just one but two domains—law and economy—which substantially increases its legitimization appeal. Another notable way in which Morawiecki strengthens legitimization of L&J's leadership is by construing his government, in the last line of (5), as a defender of "European unity." This conspicuous move is obviously meant to respond to attitudes of the vast majority of Poles who—as we saw in the previous chapter—support EU membership.

In (6), yet another ploy is used to disqualify the NS2 initiative. Describing the project as a manifestation of "Schroederism" that "is back in Europe," Morawiecki provides NS2 with essentially ideological traits that detract from perception of the project as a purely economic enterprise. At the linguistic and specifically word-formation level, this involves the use of the "-ism" suffix, a morphological ending that typically connotes abstract, often ideologically charged, concepts and ideas. The inclusion of this ending in "Schroederism" evokes associations with a specific practice, system, or philosophy (including political philosophies such as socialism or capitalism), all of which can be interpreted in ideological terms. This in turn invites ideological interpretations drawing on different associations triggered by the root word, that is, "Schroeder," which denotes a former German chancellor.[7] Notably, some of these associations turn out extremely consequential for the interpretation of "Schroederism" as a political stance, such as the employment of Gerhard Schroeder, in 2017, as the chairman of the Russian energy company Rosneft. Emerging from the above picture is Morawiecki's goal in coining the entire "Schroederism" phrase—it is to suggest a threatening possibility of Germany (and thus also EU) becoming politically dependent on Russia, as a result of the existing business connections. Making such a warning Morawiecki further strengthens the image of Poland as an active supporter of European interests.

6.2. How a Pipeline Becomes the Lifeline

Criticism of the NS2 project by the L&J government means simultaneously a defense of the existing gas transit routes, particularly the Yamal Corridor.[8] In this argument, L&J leaders often resort to figurative language, such as conceptual metaphor. The most frequent metaphoric conceptualizations involve the basic perception of STATE as a PERSON (cf. 1.4.2) and, following from this basic construal, viewing ECONOMY of the state in terms of its HEALTH:

(7) Plans for future gas transit routes to bypass Poland pose a major threat to our country's economic health. (Jarosław Kaczyński, November 18, 2018)

(8) Reliable supplies of energy are Poland's lifeline to the world economy and global markets. (PM Mateusz Morawiecki at the World Economic Forum in Davos, January 23, 2019)

(9) We cannot let NS2 destroy plans for expansion of the Yamal Corridor project, which has been our main economic lifeline in the past 20 years. (Foreign Minister Jacek Czaputowicz at the World Economic Forum in Davos, January 23, 2019)

The aforementioned examples are excerpts from speeches of L&J politicians that were given at a November 2018 parliamentary session in Poland (7) and during a plenary session of the 2019 World Economic Forum in Davos, Switzerland (8–9). The excerpt from Jarosław Kaczyński's speech illustrates the prominence of metaphor in L&J's "gas discourse" in general. Overall, in 2018 texts alone, there are 34 examples of the use of the ECONOMY is HEALTH scenario, 27 of which serve—like (7)—to defend the rationale for the existing gas transit arrangements. The other two excerpts, from speeches by Mateusz Morawiecki and Jacek Czaputowicz in Davos, demonstrate the pragmatics of the ECONOMY is HEALTH metaphor, showcasing creative ways in which L&J leaders use it to raise the emotive appeal of their argument.[9] Both texts represent an attempt to establish a sense of criticality of the moment, while Czaputowicz's text includes, also, an indication of counterresponse. Interestingly, both statements make use of the same metaphoric item, "lifeline," to perform their functions. This is, however, not (or not entirely, at least) a lexical coincidence. As a matter of fact, "lifeline" appears as many as fourteen times in the mentioned 2018 corpus—always in texts supporting the Yamal project.

It must be noted that the use of "lifeline" in metaphoric phrases defining ECONOMY in terms of HEALTH has a long history in political discourse. The most famous example is, arguably, George H. W. Bush's remark, "he is sitting on our economic lifeline," referring to Saddam Hussein's occupation of the US ally Kuwait (and, crucially, its oil fields) between July and December 1990. Made at a White House press briefing in early August (1990), the comment had received enormous attention in the media and was discussed by thousands of political commentators all around the globe. As noted by Lakoff (1991), the majority of experts viewed Bush's words as a proof of political calculation and his sheer economic (rather than humanitarian) rationale for going to war against Iraq.[10] Lakoff (1991) also observes that such a popularity and broad circulation of the comment can be attributed specifically to its inclusion of the "lifeline" metaphor. From a rhetorical perspective, the "lifeline" phrase possesses a substantial potential for recontextualization and further use in new linguistic and political contexts. This is because the "lifeline" item is, in propaganda theoretical terms, easily "detachable" and "shareable"; the text that carries it (i.e., Bush's remark) is easily extractable from the main discourse (i.e., the briefing) and readily entextualizable in a new piece of text (Urban 1996: 23). As such, the phrase reveals a considerable "rhetorical velocity"—an ability to travel through potentially infinite propagandistic channels, involving infinite numbers of recipients (Ridolfo and De Voss 2009). Crucially, the velocity feature means that many of these recipients (such as the media) are happy to redistribute the phrase in their own interest, for instance, because it echoes their political position and opinions. Of course, the "lifeline" metaphor is not unique in possessing such propagandistic properties, but, according to Lakoff (1991), its appeal to vital body functions as the main source of the metaphoric projection makes the resulting expression particularly effective.

Returning to the statements of Morawiecki and Czaputowicz, of course, it cannot be proven beyond all doubt that their use of the "lifeline" metaphor represents a strategic, premeditated rhetorical choice. It cannot be determined, either, to what extent such a choice, if indeed strategic, would have reflected the speakers' awareness of Bush's remark. It is intriguing, however, that this rather complex metaphor appears in statements made directly in the English language, by non-native speakers who actually have been demonstrating average English-language skills on other international occasions. Assuming that Morawiecki and Czaputowicz's metaphoric use of "lifeline" *is* a premeditated linguistic choice, it should be considered an extremely clever rhetorical (and political) move. This is because metaphoric phrases defining ECONOMY in terms of HEALTH are abundant in Polish political discourse, yet always attracting great attention of the main media players and being redistributed widely through all kinds of political communication channels (Bralczyk 2007). Thus, in making use of the "lifeline" metaphor Morawiecki and Czaputowicz show their ability to anticipate a future "trajectory" of the phrase that is favorable to them. The main characteristic of this trajectory is the presence, at different sections of the trajectory, of different parties—politicians, media, ordinary people—which are willing to recompose and circulate the phrase further, in their own interest.

The use of the "lifeline" metaphor in texts (8) and (9) is, finally, a promising attempt to enhance the dynamics of processes affecting entities involved in the conceptualization of Polish economy in terms of health, particularly the underlying STATE entity, that is, Poland. Thanks to the metaphor, the construal of threat to Poland's "economic health" receives a sense of urgency that endorses a call for response from international bodies, especially the EU. For the speakers in (8) and (9) such a response means, first of all, having Russia and Germany abandon the NS2 project and, second, providing support for the initiative of the Yamal pipeline extension. The "lifeline" metaphor reveals thus a value that compares to many linguistic items involved in the process of proximization—for instance the items responsible for enacting temporal proximization and symbolic centralization of the present frame as the moment to react to the envisaged threat (cf. 1.4.3).

That said, one should regard economy metaphors, as well as other instances of L&J's NS2 rhetoric as a discourse developed primarily for the home audience. Its ominous visions of exclusion and economic decline are inextricably linked to threats of highest political caliber, such as loss of political sovereignty to European superpowers, especially Russia and Germany. In their consistent construal of these two countries as the main source of the threat, Law & Justice strikes a very raw chord, activating popular fears that go back several decades, to the Second World War and the postwar communist period. Cynical as it seems, this strategy proves effective in eliciting support for the L&J party, a self-proclaimed "only defender of the rights and dignity of Polish people in Europe," in Kaczyński's words.[11] At the same time, fronts are being opened for new battles such as, recently, over Poland's share in the European freight and logistics market, which the L&J government has described as "unbecoming for a large and proud country in the heart of Europe."[12] The conceptual and discursive ways in which L&J leaders meet these new conflicts remain, however, exactly the same, including threat generation and fear appeal, and, in the end, a firm commitment to resolve what is often an own-produced crisis.

Concluding Remarks

This book has shown that the discourse of Law & Justice and its government in Poland reveals in many ways the main features of populist style as defined by leading studies in discourse and communication research, linguistics, social psychology, and political science. Positioning itself as a staunch opponent of "unpatriotic elites" and cosmopolitan liberalism together with its globalist economic policies, L&J claims to remain, home and abroad, on guard of "ordinary people," their national identity and Christian traditions. This stance entails a harsh antiestablishment rhetoric that conceptualizes the established elites—whether in Poland or in the EU—as essentially self-interested, arrogant, exploitative, and, as the NS2 case has demonstrated, treacherous. Crucially, L&J's discourse construes the party opponents as enemies, rather than as rivals. The delegitimization of political enemies involves, at conceptual and discursive levels, a firm *Them* vs. *Us* (and not just *Us* and *Them*) distinction, performed by a variety of linguistic means. The enactment of such a distinction is critical for the subsequent acts—generating a threat, exerting coercion, and, eventually, obtaining policy legitimization.

The generation of conflict and crisis is thus an inherent feature of L&J's policy and L&J's discourse. This, again, is not something unique. We have seen from the examples of other European discourses—UK's Brexit discourse, the discourse of ethnic minorities in Balkan states, the M5S party discourse in Italy—that the ideological, political, or geopolitical kinds of social divide arising in crisis conditions are all highly instrumental in effective performance of threat-based leadership. The uniqueness of Law & Justice's leadership, and its discursive manifestations, lies, however, in the essentially strategic character of crisis management. Unlike in Hungary, Italy, Romania, Bulgaria, and other countries where social or political crises tend to be exploited by certain groups and parties to further their political goals, L&J has made conflict and crisis, intentionally, an integral part of political agenda and policymaking. This can be seen not only from the ever-increasing number of conflict domains in which the L&J government is involved, but also in the directions to which L&J leaders orient themselves (often misfortunately, as it seems) in their new discourse. As this book is being finished, Law & Justice has chosen, quite surprisingly yet in a manifestly deliberate way, to meet its declining approval ratings with tightening abortion laws, thus undermining sociopolitical and legal compromise that has been in place for the past twenty-five years.

The very recent domains of conflict and the ways in which various arising crises are handled are more and more alarming. As Poles reel under the second wave of the Covid-19 pandemic, the government has seen its chance to bounce back from popularity losses, launching several obviously propagandistic projects such as a mammoth temporary hospital at the National Stadium in Warsaw, proudly named as "National Hospital." As of today, the hospital remains nearly empty for largely unknown "technical" reasons, generating sky-high costs covered at the expense of other hospitals and medical centers in Warsaw. L&J's discourse supporting such projects is at the same time a discourse of enmification and exclusion targeted at their opponents and thus L&J's political opponents in general. While it follows, in technical terms, the same patterns as other kinds of discourse described in this book, its conscious drawing upon matters of health, life, and death is quite unprecedented, evidencing L&J's intention to exploit any issues that seem beneficial from the main perspective of political propaganda and coercion.

Altogether, it is difficult to say how long L&J's discourse continues to generate popular support for the party and the government. While L&J's current approval ratings are at an all-time low since 2015, they are still higher than the support for opposition parties, such as the Civic Platform, the biggest rivals of L&J in the past fifteen years. Interestingly, even though recent public appearances of L&J politicians and the way the party reacts to emerging social crises are considered increasingly awkward by political experts, there are no trendlines in the polls posing a serious threat to L&J's leadership. For discourse analytical projects such as the present book this may mean two things. On the one hand, there are some excellent interdisciplinary tools that can say what features of populist discourse make it an effective leadership discourse. On the other hand, the same excellent tools, informed by all kinds of social and geopolitical factors, premises, and contexts, are virtually unable, as yet, to prescribe limitations of such a discourse, its "expiry date" as a policy instrument. If discourse research and critical discourse studies, in particular, keep up with their view of discourse and discourse analysis as not only reflection or description but also scholarly prediction of sociopolitical reality and change, more work is needed at the intersection of linguistics, discourse analysis, and social sciences. The "difficult case" of Law & Justice is an inviting prompt for such research.

It seems that, regardless of what empirical directions are taken, populist studies are yet to make more of the linguistic side of discourse analysis. This may mean distancing, at least to some extent, from the current conception of populism as an ideology and ideological style and adopting a more restricted, but at the same time more rigorous, perspective of populism as a pragmatic and language style. Apparently, most current approaches to populism, such as Norris and Inglehart (2018, cf. chapter 3) or Mudde and Kaltwasser (2017), see it in broad terms of an ideology that uses discourse as well as other means to split the populace into two and only two groups—"the elite" and "the people"—pitting these groups against each other and assigning moral rights and political powers to the latter. This minimal definition provides few criteria for a linguistic study of populism. It allows for some clear predictions concerning lexicon and semantics: we expect mention, in a text, of "people" and "elite," contrasts between "us" and "them," and so on. However, it does not really allow for hypotheses about populist pragmatics, let alone populist syntax or populist word-formation. This is because its focus is on *what* is said—about the elite and the people—rather than on *who* says it. If we seek to specify more truly linguistic features of populism and populist style, this personal context must be properly accounted for. For example, a very recent work on Donald Trump's language by Schneider and Eitelmann (2020) makes great strides in populist discourse analysis, adding to the existing criteria of populist style from the perspective of rhetorical self-orientation and idiosyncratic properties of lexical choices. Schneider and Eitelmann (2020) show that some of the central characteristics of populist style may need revisiting in the light of personality traits and individual predispositions of the speaker. For instance, certain lexical and narrative properties of Trump's discourse such as multiple self-mentions and personal stories shed a very special light on the populist core argument that politics should be an expression of the will of the people. In Trump's argument, people's will is important but, as Schneider and Eitelmann (2020) demonstrate, even more important is the will of the leader, who, because of his qualities, is entitled to act on behalf of the people. This naturally leads to the consideration of how the leader's will is communicated, in linguistic terms, to be consistent with the popular will. We have given several examples of such new analytical vistas in the present book, but a more comprehensive—and less Anglocentric—study is still needed to account for various populist styles around the globe that diverge from their European prototypes.

Notes

Chapter 1

1 In fact, there are works (e.g., Chilton 2014) that use the terms *discourse* and *deictic space theory* interchangeably.
2 A more detailed account of British (anti-)immigration discourse follows in Chapter 5, Section 5.1.1.
3 The interview took place only three days after an Islamic terrorist attack, in which a truck was deliberately driven into crowds celebrating the Bastille Day 2016 on the Promenade des Anglais in Nice, France, killing 84 people and injuring 434.
4 For a more extensive analysis of this interview and Farage's Brexit discourse, see Chapter 5 (Section 5.1.1).

Chapter 2

1 The agreement signed on January 1, 1947, by the US Secretary of State James F. Byrnes and the British Foreign Secretary Ernest Bevin, providing for the full economic integration of the US and the UK zones of occupation in Germany.
2 United Nations Relief and Rehabilitation Administration.
3 The operation at Mai Lai took place on March 16, 1968. A "search-and-destroy" military operation by name, it left more than 500 Vietnamese civilians killed by US forces.
4 The Katyn massacre was a series of mass executions of about 22,000 Polish military officers and intelligentsia carried out by the Soviet secret police in April and May 1940.
5 Family 500+ is a government program under which parents receive PLN 500 a month for the second and each next child, no matter how much they earn. Introduced in March 2016, it is considered realization of the Law & Justice's main promise of the 2015 parliamentary campaign.

6 Nord Stream is a system of offshore natural gas pipelines from Russia to Germany, bypassing Poland as well as other Central European countries. The project, pursued since 2011, has been opposed by most countries of Central and Eastern Europe as well as the United States, because of concerns that it would increase Russia's influence in the region.

7 Unless indicated otherwise, all excerpts from texts in the corpus are the author's translations from Polish.

Chapter 3

1 The "Round Table order" ["układ Okrągłego Stołu"] refers to the political result of negotiations that took place in Poland between the ruling communist party and the opposition in February–April 1989. As has been mentioned in Chapter 2, these talks were a key element in the collapse of the communist regime and a smooth transition to democracy. The Law & Justice party has been very critical of the talks, calling them "a deal" with communists.

2 This phrase appears as many as seventy-eight times in the corpus. It is used sixty-eight times by Kaczyński himself and ten times by other L&J politicians.

3 Nouns, verbs, as well as noun and verb phrases. Included are the items whose number is higher than 100.

4 At the time of the speech, the Constitutional Tribunal consisted (until late 2016) largely of judges elected by the Civic Platform majority during the previous parliamentary term. After the 2015 elections, Kaczyński deemed it "the stronghold of everything in Poland that is bad" (Kaczyński, November 6, 2015). The speech was part of a rally called by the L&J party to mobilize support for a bill making possible early termination of offices of the "CP judges," as Kaczyński called them.

5 Grzegorz Schetyna was leader of the Civic Platform in the years 2015–19.

6 In a recent analysis of metaphor in Donald Trump's presidential discourse, Koth (2020) describe some further pragmatic qualities of the POLITICS IS WAR scenario. Namely, the sense of urgency associated with the scenario sanctions simple solutions proposed by the leader. This in turn frees the leader from the obligation to provide evidence or justification for his or her policies. It also allows him or her to dismiss or ignore argument that runs counter to these policies. Koth's (2020) analysis reveals a remarkable degree of similarity between Trump and Kaczyński when it comes to exploiting the aforementioned possibilities.

7   Symbolizing Poland's national flag, white and red are the colors of Polish outfits at international competitions. For example, Polish soccer team plays in white jerseys, red shorts, and white socks.
8   Minister of Family, Labor and Social Policy between November 2015 and June 2019.
9   The CP rule between 2007 and 2015.
10 Minister of the Interior and Administration between January 2018 and June 2019.
11 A phrase used by Donald Trump in an election campaign speech in Phoenix, Arizona, on October 29, 2016.

Chapter 4

1   The Venice Commission (formally: The European Commission for Democracy through Law) is an advisory body of the Council of Europe, composed of independent experts in the field of constitutional law. Its primary task is to assist and advise individual countries in constitutional matters in order to improve functioning of democratic institutions and the protection of human rights.
2   The eighteen-month period of the first government of the L&J party.
3   Kornel Morawiecki in an interview for the TVP1 public television channel, November 3, 2015.
4   For instance in his interview for TVP2 on December 20, 2015.
5   A recent study by Egbert and Biber (2020) demonstrates presence of a similar conceptual mechanism in Donald Trump's presidential discourse, contesting morality of people opposing Trump's policies by calling them "crooked opponents." As argued by Egbert and Biber (2020), the concept of "crooked opponents" is juxtaposed against the notion of the "Great Movement," which applies to Trump's supporters. Apart from being a reference term, "Great Movement" connotes a momentous and positive change of social order, which reveals another analogy with L&J's discourse and its "Good Change" ("Dobra Zmiana") catchword.
6   Underline by P.C.
7   Underline by P.C.
8   See also the discussion in Chapter 2, Section 2.2.
9   Cf. note 1.
10 Julia Pitera, Barbara Kudrycka, Michał Boni, and Danuta Hübner were four of the fourteen Polish MEPs voting in favor of the EP resolution.

11 Waldemar Żurek and Igor Tuleya are top representatives of the Iustitia Association of judges, opposing L&J's reform of the judiciary.
12 Adopted May 16, 2011.
13 MEP Angel Dzhambazki for BNT Novini, April 14, 2020.
14 PM Mihai Ungureanu for the *Times*, October 3, 2012.
15 Jurnalul Național, May 20, 2013.

Chapter 5

1 It has been broadly documented in post-2016 research that immigration (and mainly *anti*-immigration) topics and narratives pervading the Brexit debate were much influential on the evolution of attitudes surrounding the Brexit referendum and, consequently, on its results. Specifically, a bulk of the anti-immigration discourse in 2013–16 was instrumental in instilling a sense of public uncertainty and ever-growing anxiety, inspiring isolationist postures and xenophobic attitudes, which found their outlet on the day of the referendum (Tournier-Sol 2017; Koller, Kopf, and Miglbauer 2019). A major survey designed by the National Centre for Social Research (NCSR) and performed on 3,000 UK citizens in June 2017 reveals that nearly three-quarters (73 percent) of those worried about immigration and its social effects (on security, employment, welfare, etc.) voted Leave, compared with 36 percent of those who did not identify this as a concern. It also shows, more specifically, that the longer any given voter felt EU migrants should have lived in the UK before qualifying for welfare benefits, the more likely they were to vote to leave the EU. These findings demonstrate, according to the NCSR, that Britain's vote to leave the EU was the result of widespread anti-immigration sentiment, rather than a wider dissatisfaction with EU policies or politics in general (see also: https://www.independent.co.uk/news/uk/home-news/brexit-latest-news-leave-eu-immigration-main-reason-european-union-survey-a7811651.html).

2 As such, the discussion reverses the order so far; it begins its inquiry not with Poland and L&J, but with another national discourse. This is to do justice to enormous geopolitical implications of Brexit campaign, and its lasting effects upon the growth of Eurosceptic, isolationist attitudes in several European countries. As documented by studies included in Staiger and Martill (2018) the Brexit example surfaces in 2017–18 discourses of virtually all of the most important nationalist far-right parties and their leaders in Europe: Kaczyński in Poland, Orban in Hungary, Salvini in Italy, Gauland in Germany, Wilders in

the Netherlands, among others. Similarities are not just conceptual. In many of these discourses, argue Staiger and Martill (2018), specific lexical patterns (for instance metaphoric structures) follow up on the British originals, with the aim of accomplishing similar coercive effects.

3 The distinction between the "first" and "second" phases of Farage's Brexit rhetoric is a conclusion from research involving thirty public speeches made by Nigel Farage between February 2014 and November 2016. Though this research and the finding should be described as essentially qualitative, Staiger and Martill (2018) postulate an identical distinction on quantitative grounds, involving, for example, comparisons of frequencies of lexical markers of affect and engagement (cf. Martin and White 2005).

4 Including, namely, example (8), a few weeks after the referendum, in which time Farage's discourse continues to demonstrate the main features of his anti-immigration rhetoric. See also Chapter 1 (Section 1.4.3).

5 Farage's comment in (8) was made three days after an Islamic terrorist attack, in which a truck was deliberately driven into crowds celebrating the Bastille Day 2016 on the Promenade des Anglais in Nice, France, killing 84 people and injuring 434.

6 Farage refers to a series of coordinated terrorist attacks that occurred on November 13, 2015, in Paris, leaving 130 people dead and another 413 injured.

7 In fact, the EC proposal included the figure "€250,000."

8 Just like Nigel Farage in example (8), Mariusz Błaszczak (the then Minister of the Interior) makes his statement precisely three days after an Islamic terrorist attack in Nice, France, in which eighty-four people were killed after a truck was driven into crowds celebrating Bastille Day on July 14 (see note #5, this chapter).

9 Błaszczak refers here to the Civic Platform liberal party, ruling Poland between 2007 and 2015.

10 Jarosław Kaczyński in an interview for *Gazeta Polska*, January 24, 2016.

11 https://ec.europa.eu/commfrontoffice/publicopinion/index.cfm.

Chapter 6

1 Liquefied natural gas (LNG) is natural gas that has been cooled down to liquid form for ease and safety of non-pressurized storage or transport.

2 At the time of the report, Britain was still a member of the EU.

3 Russia's Federal Security Service.

4 Pellegrini held the office between March 2018 and March 2020.

5. The Visegrád Group—Visegrád Four, or V4—is a cultural and political alliance of four countries of Central Europe—the Czech Republic, Hungary, Poland, and Slovakia—to advance cooperation in military, cultural, economic, and energy matters.
6. Kaczyński refers here to the Locarno Treaties, which were seven agreements signed at Locarno, Switzerland, in October 1925. The Treaties aimed to secure the postwar territorial settlement and normalize relations with the defeated German Reich (the Weimar Republic). They divided borders in Europe into two categories: western, which were guaranteed in the provisions of the Treaties, and eastern borders of Germany with Poland, which were open for possible revision.
7. Gerhard Schroeder, Chancellor of Germany from 1998 to 2005.
8. Operating since 1997, Yamal Corridor is a natural gas pipeline that carries gas from the Yamal Peninsula region of western Siberia to European consumers. It runs from western Siberia through Russia, Belarus, and Poland, into eastern Germany, where it connects with the Western European gas grid.
9. Both speeches were given in English.
10. The war, known as the First Gulf War, started on January 17, 1991, with an aerial and naval bombardment of Iraqi troops in Kuwait.
11. Jarosław Kaczyński for Gazeta Polska, September 12, 2020.
12. Mateusz Morawiecki for Gazeta Polska, November 17, 2020.

Bibliography

Abdi, R. and A. Basarati (2018), "Legitimation in Discourse and Communication Revisited: A Critical View towards Legitimizing Identities in Communication," *International Journal of Society, Culture & Language*, 6: 86–100.

Agh, A. (2016), "Cultural War and Reinventing the Past in Poland and Hungary: The Politics of Historical Memory in East-Central Europe," *Polish Political Science Yearbook*, 45: 32–44.

Altman, A. (2017), "How Donald Trump Is Bringing the Alt-Right to the White House," *TIME*, February 9, 2017.

Andersen, J. G. and T. Bjørklund (1990), "Structural Changes and New Cleavages: The Progress Parties in Denmark and Norway," *Acta Sociologica*, 33: 195–217.

Arendt, H. (1958), *The Human Condition*, Chicago: University of Chicago Press.

Angermuller, J., D. Maingueneau, and R. Wodak, eds. (2014), *The Discourse Studies Reader: Main Currents in Theory and Analysis*, Amsterdam: John Benjamins.

Aronson, E. (1969), "The Theory of Cognitive Dissonance: A Current Perspective," in L. Berkowitz (ed.), *Advances in Experimental Social Psychology, Vol. 4*, 1–34, New York: Academic Press.

Arppe, A., G. Gilquin, D. Glynn, M. Hilpert, and A. Zeschel (2010), "Cognitive Corpus Linguistics: Five Points of Debate on Current Theory and Methodology," *Corpora*, 5: 1–27.

Axelrod, R. (1984), *The Evolution of Cooperation*, New York: Basic Books.

Bandura, A. (1986), *Social Foundations of Thought and Action: A Social Cognitive Theory*, Englewood Cliffs, NJ: Prentice Hall.

Bar-Hillel, Y. (1954), "Indexical Expressions," *Mind*, 63: 359–79.

Bartha, P. (2010), *By Parallel Reasoning: The Construction and Evaluation of Analogical Arguments*, Oxford: Oxford University Press.

Bednarek, M. (2006), *Evaluation in Media Discourse: Analysis of a Newspaper Corpus*, London: Continuum.

Billig, M. (1996), *Arguing and Thinking: A Rhetorical Approach to Social Psychology*, Cambridge: Cambridge University Press.

Bobba, G. (2018), "Social Media Populism: Features and 'likeability' of Lega Nord Communication on Facebook," *European Political Science*, 18: 11–23.

Borger, J. (2002), "Rumsfeld Offered Help to Saddam," *Guardian*, December 31, 2002.

Bouwmeester, M. C. and J. Oosterhaven (2017), "Economic Impacts of Natural Gas Flow Disruptions between Russia and the EU," *Energy Policy*, 106: 288–97.

Bracciale, R. and A. Martella (2017), "Define the Populist Political Communication Style: The Case of Italian Political Leaders on Twitter," *Information, Communication & Society*, 20: 1310–29.

Bralczyk, J. (2007), *O języku propagandy i polityki*, Warsaw: Trio.

Buehler, K. (1934), *Sprachtheorie: Die Darstellungsfunktion der Sprache*, Stuttgart: Fischer.

Bunikowski, D. (2018), "The Constitutional Crisis in Poland, Schmittian Questions and Kaczyński's Political and Legal Philosophy," *Journal of Contemporary European Studies*, 26: 285–307.

Cameron, D. (2013), "EU Speech at Bloomberg," Cabinet Office release, January 23, 2013. https://www.gov.uk/government/speeches/eu-speech-at-bloomberg

Cap, P. (2006), *Legitimization in Political Discourse: A Cross-disciplinary Perspective on the Modern US War Rhetoric*, Newcastle: Cambridge Scholars Press.

Cap, P. (2008), "Towards the Proximization Model of the Analysis of Legitimization in Political Discourse," *Journal of Pragmatics*, 40: 17–41.

Cap, P. (2010), "Axiological Aspects of Proximization," *Journal of Pragmatics*, 42: 392–407.

Cap, P. (2013), *Proximization: The Pragmatics of Symbolic Distance Crossing*, Amsterdam: John Benjamins.

Cap, P. (2017), *The Language of Fear: Communicating Threat in Public Discourse*, Basingstoke: Palgrave-Macmillan.

Cap, P. (2019), "'Britain Is Full to Bursting Point!' Immigration Themes in the Brexit Discourse of the UK Independence Party," in V. Koller, S. Kopf, and M. Miglbauer (eds.), *Discourses of Brexit*, 69–85, London: Routledge.

Cap, P. (2021), "Alternative Futures in Political Discourse," *Discourse & Society*, 32.

Cap, P. and U. Okulska, eds. (2013), *Analyzing Genres in Political Communication: Theory in Practice*, Amsterdam: John Benjamins.

Charteris-Black, J. (2005), *Politicians and Rhetoric: The Persuasive Power of Metaphor*, Basingstoke: Palgrave-Macmillan.

Chilton, P. (2004), *Analysing Political Discourse: Theory and Practice*, London: Routledge.

Chilton, P. (2005), "Discourse Space Theory: Geometry, Brain and Shifting Viewpoints," *Annual Review of Cognitive Linguistics*, 3: 78–116.

Chilton, P. (2010), "From Mind to Grammar: Coordinate Systems, Prepositions, Constructions," in V. Evans and P. Chilton (eds.), *Language, Cognition and Space: The State of the Art and New Directions*, 640–71, London: Equinox.

Chilton, P. (2011), "Deictic Space Theory (DST): The Fundamental Theory and its Applications," Paper presented at the 42nd Poznań Linguistic Meeting, Poznań, May 1–3, 2011.

Chilton, P. (2014), *Language, Space and Mind: The Conceptual Geometry of Linguistic Meaning*, Cambridge: Cambridge University Press.

Chovanec, J. (2010), "Legitimation through Differentiation: Discursive Construction of Jacques Le Worm Chirac as an Opponent to Military Action," in P. Cap and U. Okulska (eds.), *Perspectives in Politics and Discourse*, 61–82, Amsterdam: John Benjamins.

Cienki, A., B. Kaal and, I. Maks (2010), "Mapping World View in Political Texts Using Discourse Space Theory: Metaphor as an Analytical Tool," Paper presented at the RaAM 8 conference, Amsterdam, July 10–12, 2010.

Cordell, K. and K. Jajecznik, eds. (2015), *The Transformation of Nationalism in Central and Eastern Europe: Ideas and Structures*, Warsaw: Warsaw University Press.

Coser, L. (1975), *The Idea of Social Structure: Papers in Honor of Robert K. Merton*, New York: Harcourt Brace Jovanovich.

Cosmides, L. (1989), "The Logic of Social Exchange: Has Natural Selection Shaped How Humans Reason? Studies within the Wason Selection Task," *Cognition*, 31: 187–276.

Cramer, P. (2013), "Sick Stuff: A Case Study of Controversy in a Constitutive Attitude," *Rhetoric Society Quarterly*, 43: 177–201.

Cullen, P. and E. Korolczuk (2019), "Challenging Abortion Stigma: Framing Abortion in Ireland and Poland," *Sexual and Reproductive Health Matters*, 27: 6–19.

Demetriou, D. (2018), "Welfare Restrictions and "Benefit Tourists": Representations and Evaluations of EU Migrants in the UK," *Communications*, 43: 379–401.

Dunmire, P. (2011), *Projecting the Future through Political Discourse: The Case of the Bush Doctrine*, Amsterdam: John Benjamins.

Egbert, J. and D. Biber (2020), "'It's Just Words, Folks, It's Just Words": Donald Trump's Distinctive Linguistic Style," in U. Schneider and M. Eitelmann (eds.), *Linguistic Inquiries into Donald Trump's Language: From 'Fake News' to 'Tremendous Success,'* 17–40, London: Bloomsbury.

Erman, E. (2018), "The Political Legitimacy of Global Governance and the Proper Role of Civil Society Actors," *Res Publica*, 24: 133–55.

Evans V. and P. Chilton, eds. (2010), *Language, Cognition and Space: The State of the Art and New Directions*, London: Equinox.

Festinger, L. (1957), *A Theory of Cognitive Dissonance*, Stanford, CA: Stanford University Press.

Fetzer, A. and G. Lauerbach, eds. (2007), *Political Discourse in the Media*, Amsterdam: John Benjamins.

Flowerdew, J. and J. Richardson, eds. (2018), *The Routledge Handbook of Critical Discourse Studies*, London: Routledge.

Fauconnier, G. and M. Turner (2002), *The Way We Think: Conceptual Blending and the Mind's Hidden Complexities*, New York: Basic Books.

Filardo Llamas, L. (2010), "Discourse Worlds in Northern Ireland: The Legitimisation of the 1998 Agreement," in K. Hayward and C. O'Donnell (eds.), *Political Discourse and Conflict Resolution: Debating Peace in Northern Ireland*, 62–76, London: Routledge.

Galasińska, A. and D. Galasiński, eds. (2010), *The Post-communist Condition: Public and Private Discourses of Transformation*, Amsterdam: John Benjamins.

Gardenfors, P. (2002), "Cooperation and the Evolution of Symbolic Communication," *Lund University Cognitive Studies*, 91: 1–18.

Gerő, M., P. Płucienniczak, A. Kluknavska, J. Navratil, and K. Kanellopoulos (2017), "Understanding Enemy Images in Central and Eastern European Politics," *Intersections EEJSP*, 3: 14–40.

Gomola, A. (2019), "Godly Poland in Godless Europe: Catholic-nationalist Discourse in Poland after 2004," in L. Šarić and M. Stanojević (eds.), *Metaphor, Nation and Discourse*, 75–100, Amsterdam: John Benjamins.

Gough, V. and M. Talbot (1996), "'Guilt over Games Boys Play': Coherence as a Focus for Examining the Constitution of Heterosexual Subjectivity on a Problem Page," in C. R. Caldas-Coulthard and M. Coulthard (eds.), *Texts and Practices: Readings in Critical Discourse Analysis*, 214–30, London: Routledge.

Grice, P. (1975), "Logic and Conversation," in P. Cole and J. Morgan (eds.), *Syntax and Semantics 3: Speech Acts*, 41–58, New York: Academic Press.

Groom, N. (2000), "Attribution and Averral Revisited: Three Perspectives on Manifest Intertextuality in Academic Writing," in P. Thompson (ed.), *Patterns and Perspectives: Insights into EAP Writing Practices*, 15–27, Reading: CALS.

Habermas, J. (1981), *Theorie des kommunikativen Handelns*, Frankfurt am Main: Suhrkamp.

Halliday, M. A. K. and J. R. Martin, eds. (1993), *Writing Science: Literacy and Discursive Power*, Bristol: The Falmer Press.

Hansard. (2013–14), *House of Commons Debates*, vol. 565–71. https://publications.parliament.uk/pa/cm/cmse1314.htm

Hart, C. (2010), *Critical Discourse Analysis and Cognitive Science: New Perspectives on Immigration Discourse*, Basingstoke: Palgrave-Macmillan.

Hart, C. (2014), *Discourse, Grammar and Ideology: Functional and Cognitive Perspectives*, London: Bloomsbury.

Hart, C. (2018), "Cognitive Linguistic Critical Discourse Studies," in J. Flowerdew and J. Richardson (eds.), *The Routledge Handbook of Critical Discourse Studies*, 77–91, London: Routledge.

Hart, C. and P. Cap, eds. (2014), *Contemporary Critical Discourse Studies*, London: Bloomsbury.

Hartman, R. (2002), *The Knowledge of Good: Critique of Axiological Reason*, Amsterdam: Rodopi.

Hayden, M. (2018), *The Assault on Intelligence: American National Security in an Age of Lies*, New York: Penguin.

Hehn, P. (2005), *A Low Dishonest Decade: The Great Powers, Eastern Europe, and the Economic Origins of World War II, 1930-1941*, London: Continuum.

Hockett, C. (1960), "The Origin of Speech," *Scientific American*, 203: 88-96.

Horn, L. (2004), "Implicature," in L. Horn and G. Ward (eds.), *The Handbook of Pragmatics*, 3-28, Oxford: Blackwell.

Hunt, J. (2003), *The Inaugural Addresses of the Presidents*, New York: Gramercy Books.

Huntington, S. (2004), *Who Are We: The Challenges to America's National Identity*, New York: Simon & Schuster.

Jacobsson, K. (2015), *Urban Grassroots Movements in Central and Eastern Europe*, New York: Ashgate.

Jary, M. (2010), *Assertion*, Basingstoke: Palgrave-Macmillan.

Jaworski, A. and D. Galasiński (1998), "The Last Romantic Hero: Lech Wałęsa's Image-building in TV Presidential Debates," *TEXT*, 18: 525-44.

Johnson, M. (1987), *The Body in the Mind: The Bodily Basis of Meaning, Imagination, and Reason*, Chicago: University of Chicago Press.

Jowett, G. and V. O'Donnell (1992), *Propaganda and Persuasion*, Newbury Park, CA: Sage.

Jowett, G. and V. O'Donnell (2015), *Propaganda and Persuasion* (2nd ed.), Newbury Park, CA: Sage.

Kamiński, B. (2016), *Fear Management: Foreign Threats in the Postwar Polish Propaganda – The Influence and the Reception of the Communist Media (1944-1956)*, Ph.D. dissertation, European University Institute, Florence.

Kaneva, N. and D. Popescu (2014), "'We are Romanian, not Roma': Nation Branding and Postsocialist Discourses of Alterity," *Communication, Culture & Critique*, 7: 506-23.

Karv, H. (2012), *Committed to democracy? A discourse analysis of the European Parliament*, Unpublished thesis.

Kemp-Welch, T. (2008), *Poland under Communism: A Cold War History*, Cambridge: Cambridge University Press.

Kersten, K. (1984), *Narodziny systemu władzy: Polska 1943-1948*, Warszawa: Kantor Wydawniczy SAWW.

Koller, V. (2014), "Applying Social Cognition Research to Critical Discourse Studies: The Case of Collective Identities," in C. Hart and P. Cap (eds.), *Contemporary Critical Discourse Studies*, 147-66, London: Bloomsbury.

Koller, V., S. Kopf, and M. Miglbauer, eds. (2019), *Discourses of Brexit*, London: Routledge.

Kopytowska, M., Ł. Grabowski, and J. Woźniak (2017), "Mobilizing against the Other: Cyberhate, Refugee Crisis and Proximization," in M. Kopytowska (ed.), *Contemporary Discourses of Hate and Radicalism across Space and Genres*, 30–55, Amsterdam: John Benjamins.

Koth, A. (2020), "'Either We WIN this Election, or We Are Going to LOSE this Country!': Trump's Warlike Competition Metaphor," in U. Schneider and M. Eitelmann (eds.), *Linguistic Inquiries into Donald Trump's Language: From 'Fake News' to 'Tremendous Success,'* 155–72, London: Bloomsbury.

Królikowska, P. (2015), *Discourse of Conflict as Political Genre*, Łódź: University of Łódź Press.

Krzyżanowski, M. (2009), "On the 'Europeanisation' of Identity Constructions in Polish Political Discourse after 1989," in A. Galasińska and M. Krzyżanowski (eds.), *Discourse and Transformation in Central and Eastern Europe. Language and Globalization*, 95–113, London: Palgrave-Macmillan.

Kwiecień, R. (2006), "The Primacy of European Union Law over National Law Under the Constitutional Treaty," in P. Dann and M. Rynkowski (eds.), *The Unity of the European Constitution*, 67–86, Berlin: Springer.

Lakoff, G. (1991), "Metaphor and War: The Metaphor System Used to Justify War in the Gulf," *Peace Research*, 23: 25–32.

Lakoff, G. and M. Johnson (1980), *Metaphors We Live By*, Chicago: University of Chicago Press.

Lefebvre, H. (1974), *La Production de l'espace*, Paris: Anthropos.

Leszczyński, A. (2018), "Anty-unijne wzmożenie PiS," OKO.press. https://oko.press/antyunijne-wzmozenie-pis-wracaja-opowiesci-o-targowicy-i-szczucie-niemcem-o-co-chodzi-tym-razem/

Levinson, S. (2000), *Presumptive Meanings: The Theory of Generalized Conversational Implicature*, Cambridge, MA: The MIT Press.

Levinson, S. (2003), *Space in Language and Cognition: Explorations in Cognitive Diversity*, Cambridge: Cambridge University Press.

Lowe, K. (2012), *Savage Continent: Europe in the Aftermath of World War II*, New York: St. Martin's Press.

Łazor, J. and W. Morawski (2016), "The Memory of Communist Poland in the Third Polish Republic: A Tentative Systematisation," *Public Policy Studies*, 4: 33–57.

Machiavelli, N. (1532/2003), *The Prince*. Middlesex: Penguin Books.

Mann, W. and S. Thompson (1988), "Rhetorical Structure Theory: A Theory of Text Organization," *Text*, 8: 243–81.

Marlin, R. (2013), *Propaganda and the Ethics of Persuasion*, Toronto: Broadview Press.

Martin, J.R. and R. Wodak, eds. (2003), *Re/reading the Past: Critical and Functional Perspectives on Time and Value*, Amsterdam: John Benjamins.

Martin, J. R. and P. White (2005), *The Language of Evaluation: Appraisal in English*, Basingstoke: Palgrave-Macmillan.

Mazzoleni, G. and R. Bracciale (2018), "Socially Mediated Populism: The Communicative Strategies of Political Leaders on Facebook," *Palgrave Communications*, 4. https://doi.org/10.1057/s41599-018-0104-x

McGarry, A. (2017), *Romaphobia: The Last Acceptable Form of Racism*, London: Zed Books.

Mizielińska, J. and A. Stasińska (2017), "'There Is Nothing like a Family': Discourses on Families of Choice in Poland," *Journal of Homosexuality*, 64: 1793–815.

Mudde, C. and C. R. Kaltwasser (2017), *Populism: A Very Short Introduction*, Oxford: Oxford University Press.

Musolff, A. (2016), *Political Metaphor Analysis: Discourse and Scenarios*, London: Bloomsbury.

Musolff, A. and J. Zinken (2009), *Metaphor and Discourse*, Basingstoke: Palgrave-Macmillan.

Myslik, B., L. Khalitova, T. Zhang, S. Tarasevich, S. Kiousis, T. Mohr, J. Y. Kim, A. Turska-Kawa, C. Carroll, and G. Golan (2019), "Two Tales of One Crash: Intergovernmental Media Relations and Agenda Building during the Smolensk Airplane Crash," *International Communication Gazette*, July 19, 2019. https://doi.org/10.1177/1748048519853766

Nicolae, V. (2013), *We Are the Roma! 1000 Years of Discrimination*, Chicago: University of Chicago Press.

Norris, P. and R. Inglehart (2018), *Cultural Backlash: Trump, Brexit and Authoritarian Populism*, Cambridge: Cambridge University Press.

Novikova, K. (2017), "'Mohair Berets': Media Representations of Elderly Right-Wing Women and Aestheticization of Age in Poland," in M. Koettig, R. Bitzan and A. Peto (eds.), *Gender and Far-Right Politics in Europe*, 207–19, Basingstoke: Palgrave-Macmillan.

Oddo, J. (2018), *The Discourse of Propaganda: Case Studies from the Persian Gulf War and the War on Terror*, University Park, PA: The PSU Press.

Pakulski, J. (2018), "Classical Elite Theory: Pareto and Weber," in H. Best and J. Higley (eds.), *The Palgrave Handbook of Elites*, 17–25, London: Palgrave-Macmillan.

Popow, M. (2015), "Postcolonial Central Europe: Between Domination and Subordination. The Example of Poland," *KULT*, 12: 96–118.

Prażmowska, A. (2010), *Poland: A Modern History*, London: I.B. Tauris & Co.

Raś, M. (2017), "Foreign and Security Policy in the Party Discourse in Poland: Main Futures," *UNISCI Journal*, 43: 117–41.

Ridolfo, J. and D. De Voss (2009), "Composing for Recomposition: Rhetorical Velocity and Delivery," *Kairos: A Journal of Rhetoric, Technology, and Pedagogy*, 13: 20–35.

Schmölz, B. (2019), "Misunderstanding, Conflict and Divisions between the Visegrad Group and the European Union – An Analytical Discourse beyond the Public Cliché of the Migration Crisis," *CES Working Papers*, 11: 22–34.

Schneider, U. and M. Eitelmann, eds. (2020), *Linguistic Inquiries into Donald Trump's Language: From "Fake News" to "Tremendous Success,"* London: Bloomsbury.

Searle, J. (1979), *Expression and Meaning: Studies in the Theory of Speech Acts*, Cambridge: Cambridge University Press

Sherif, M. and C. Hovland (1961), *Social Judgment: Assimilation and Contrast Effects in Communication and Attitude Change*, New Haven, CT: Yale University Press.

Shields, S. (2012), *The International Political Economy of Transition: Transnational Social Forces and Eastern Central Europe's Transformation*, London: Routledge.

Silberstein, S. (2004), *War of Words*, London: Routledge.

Simmel, G. (1955), *Conflict and the Web of Group Affiliations*, Glencoe, IL: Free Press.

Sofizade, J. (2019), "The 'Debate' about Poland," *Politeja* 63: 215–25.

Sperber, D. (2000), "Metarepresentations in an Evolutionary Perspective," in D. Sperber (ed.), *Metarepresentation: A Multidisciplinary Perspective*, 117–38, New York: Oxford University Press.

Staiger, U. and B. Martill, eds. (2018), *Brexit and Beyond*, London: UCL Press.

Sziklai, B., L. Koczy and D Csercsik (2019), "The Geopolitical Impact of Nord Stream 2," *USAEE Working Paper* No. 19-394. http://dx.doi.org/10.2139/ssrn.3360783

Szilágyi, A. and A. Bozóki (2015), "Playing It Again in Post-Communism: The Revolutionary Rhetoric of Viktor Orban in Hungary," *Advances in the History of Rhetoric*, 18: 153–66.

Szulecka, J. and K. Szulecki (2019), "Between Domestic Politics and Ecological Crises: (De)legitimization of Polish Environmentalism," *Environmental Politics*, 29. https://doi.org/10.1080/09644016.2019.1674541

Todd, J. (2015), *The British Self and Continental Other: A Discourse Analysis of the United Kingdom's Relationship with Europe*, Oslo: ARENA.

Tournier-Sol, K. (2017), "UKIP, the Architect of Brexit?" *The French Journal of British Studies*. https://journals.openedition.org/rfcb/1378

Urban, G. (1996), "Entextualization, Replication, Power," in M. Silverstein and G. Urban (eds.), *Natural Histories of Discourse*, 21–44, Chicago: University of Chicago Press.

Van Dijk, T. (2007), "Macro Contexts," in U. Lottgen and J. S. Sánchez (eds.), *Discourse and International Relations*, 3–26, Bern: Peter Lang.

Van Dijk, T. (2015), "Critical Discourse Analysis," in D. Tannen, H. Hamilton and D. Schiffrin (eds), *The Handbook of Discourse Analysis*, 466–85, Malden: Blackwell.

Van Eemeren, F. and R. Grootendorst (2004), *A Systematic Theory of Argumentation*, Cambridge: Cambridge University Press.

Van Leeuwen, T. and R. Wodak (1999), "Legitimizing Immigration Control: A Discourse-Historical Analysis," *Discourse Studies*, 10: 83–118.

Volkan, V. (1985), "The Need to Have Enemies and Allies: A Developmental Approach," *Political Psychology*, 6: 219–47.

Wylęgalski, A. (2019), *Solidarity-based versus liberal Poland: Jarosław Kaczynski's discourse of thin-centered populism in the light of Norman Fairclough's critical discourse analysis*, PhD dissertation, University of Tartu.

Zaremba, M. (2006), *Komunizm. Legitymizacja. Nacjonalizm. Nacjonalistyczna legitymizacja władzy komunistycznej w Polsce*, Warszawa: TRIO.

Zienkowski, J., J.-O. Östman, and J. Verschueren, eds. (2011), *Discursive Pragmatics*, Amsterdam: John Benjamins.

Zimbardo, P. and M. Leippe (1991), *The Psychology of Attitude Change and Social Influence*, New York: McGraw-Hill.

Media sources

Express Ilustrowany, December 11, 1946.
Express Ilustrowany, December 30, 1946.
Express Ilustrowany, January 20, 1947.
Express Ilustrowany, November 18, 1954.
Express Ilustrowany, June 3, 1955.
Frankfurter Allgemeine Zeitung, October 11, 2012.
Gazeta Polska, May 4, 1999.
Gazeta Polska, December 4, 2009.
Gazeta Polska, July 25, 2010.
Gazeta Polska, April 3, 2011.
Gazeta Polska, May 15, 2015.
Gazeta Polska, December 11, 2015.
Gazeta Polska, January 24, 2016.
Gazeta Polska, November 30, 2017.
Gazeta Polska, May 16, 2019.
Gazeta Polska, June 2, 2019.
Gazeta Polska, September 12, 2020.
Gazeta Polska, November 17, 2020.

Gazeta Wyborcza, July 16, 1998.
Gazeta Wyborcza, March 3, 1999.
Gazeta Wyborcza, June 3, 2003.
Gazeta Wyborcza, November 2, 2015.
Gazeta Wyborcza, May 4, 2017.
Głos Robotniczy, February 15, 1950.
Hungary Today, April 15, 2018.
Jurnalul Naţional, May 20, 2013.
Rzeczpospolita, May 18, 2004.
Szpilki, September 16, 1954.
The Times, October 3, 2012.
The Washington Post, November 3, 2015.
Trybuna Ludu, August 14, 1954.
Trybuna Ludu, February 6, 1968.
Trybuna Ludu, February 21, 1968.
Trybuna Ludu, March 6, 1969.
Trybuna Ludu, June 2, 1985.

Index

alternative futures 126, 128, 131, 133, 135
analogical reasoning 12
anti-terrorist discourse 10, 31
Article 7 1, 5, 103, 105, 113–14, 136–7, 140
assertion 17–18

Babiš, Andrej 147
BBC 31, 121, 134
Brexit 1, 3–4, 114, 120, 123–6, 128, 135, 155, 159, 162–3
  campaign 118, 125, 135
  referendum 31, 114, 117, 135, 162
Bush, George W. 7, 18

Cameron, David 115–18, 120
camp
  liberal 93
  solidarity 93, 96
cheater detection module 16, 18
Chilton, Paul 21, 23–4
Clinton, Bill 23–5
coherence 16, 89, 129, 134
Cold War 25, 44, 52
Colorado beetle 43, 54
communist regime 61–2, 160
consistency theory 15
Constitutional Tribunal 68, 136, 160
CONTAINER schema 122–4, 128
conversational implicature 17–18
Covid-19 109, 156
credibility 8, 13, 15–20, 35, 62, 69, 128–9, 134–5
critical discourse studies (CDS) 2, 21, 26, 33, 156

decommunization 47–8, 55
deictic
  center 22, 26, 30, 122
  periphery 30, 133
deictic/discourse space theory (DST) 3, 20–30, 32–3, 35, 159

delegitimization 10, 11, 35, 155
dichotomous representation 11, 93
Di Maio, Luigi 87–90
discourse space 22, 26, 28–30, 32, 86, 122
Dzhambazki, Angel 109, 162

enmification 3, 106–11, 156
evidentiality 19, 81, 129, 131, 134
exceptionalism 71, 105, 115–16, 127–8
European Parliament 5, 16, 54, 102–3, 113, 119, 121, 136, 140, 147, 149–50

Farage, Nigel 31–2, 114–15, 117–21, 124, 163
fear
  appeals 3, 30, 39, 54, 58–60, 79, 90, 118, 124, 126
  dichotomies 11, 13, 15
Festinger, Leon 15, 129
FIDESZ 2, 53, 80–3, 85, 87
Five (5) Star Movement 4, 58, 80, 86–7
flashback vision 31, 75, 77
future
  oppositional 126, 128–9, 131, 133–4, 149
  privileged 78, 128–9, 131, 134, 149

Gazprom 144, 146, 148

Habermas, Juergen 9–10
Hollande, Francois 13
Hussein, Saddam 14, 18, 152

illocutionary force 17
indexicality 11, 20
intertextuality 28
interventionist discourse 10, 12, 23
Iraq war 18
ISIS 13
isolationist 13, 115, 121, 125–6, 162

judicial reform 136, 138, 150, 154

Kennedy, John F. 17
Kosovo 23–5

latitude of acceptance 15, 60
LGBT community/groups 70, 92, 98–9
"lifeline" metaphor 152–4

Marshall Plan 42
message/text trajectory 14, 153
migration crisis 1, 5, 113–15, 130–1
modality
　absolute 129, 131, 134
　probabilistic 129, 131, 134, 149
modus ponens 18
Molotov-Ribbentrop Pact 6, 144, 150
multiculturalism 3–4, 55, 58, 127
Musolff, Andreas 26–9

national
　sovereignty rhetoric 5, 113–14, 125
　traitors 48, 92
Nazi Germany 10, 38, 150
Nice terrorist attack 32, 121, 132, 134, 159, 163
Northern League 4, 80, 86

Orban, Viktor 2, 53, 58, 80, 82–6, 88, 90, 162

pedagogy of shame 61, 63, 65
policy legitimization 3, 6, 18, 20, 28–9, 35, 45, 54, 70, 76, 79, 86, 91, 111, 126, 143, 148, 150, 155
political
　discourse analysis (PDA) 20–1
　metaphor 3, 20, 26–8, 35, 123
populism 52–3, 80–1, 157
propaganda theory 13–14
proximization
　axiological 4–5, 30–2, 74, 76, 78–9, 101, 104, 119, 132
　spatial 30–1, 78, 119, 125
　temporal 30, 76–7, 120, 154
　theory 3, 20, 29–33, 35, 40, 74

recontextualization 13–14, 20, 60, 153
refugee
　crisis 1, 5, 52, 113–15, 131
　relocation schema 1, 82, 113–14, 126–8, 130–2, 134–5
rhetorical structure theory (RST) 129

rhetorical velocity 14, 60, 90, 153
Roman Catholic Church 46, 99
Romaphobia 108
Roosevelt, Franklin D. 16
Round Table 46–7, 57–8, 61–2, 94, 160
rule of law 2, 53, 61–2, 91–4, 103, 136, 138, 140, 149–50

Salvini, Matteo 87–90, 108, 162
scenario
　conceptual 26, 66, 122
　metaphoric 29, 58, 66, 68, 86
Second World War (WWII) 3, 7, 24–5, 36–8, 52, 91–2, 98, 105, 116–17, 127, 154
September 11 (9/11) 7–8, 13, 29, 31
shareability 14, 28, 64, 153
sharing visions 9–10
shmaltsovniks 102, 105–7
Simeonov, Valeri 109, 111
Smolensk air disaster 48–9, 52, 71, 92, 97–8
social
　coercion 3, 12, 20–1, 33, 54, 104
　mobilization 3, 7, 10, 35–7, 40, 44, 54, 76
solidarity 46–7, 54, 64
source-tagging 19, 120
Soviet bloc 52, 106, 141
speech act theory 17
state legitimacy 93–6, 113

Targowica 102–7
threat construction 7–8, 21, 31, 33, 90
total opposition 57
Trump, Donald 8, 73, 81, 146, 157, 160–1

United Kingdom Independence Party (UKIP) 2, 5, 31, 114–15, 117–19, 121–2, 124–8, 135, 141

Venice Commission 91, 103, 161
Visegrád Group 53, 148, 164

weapons of mass destruction (WMD) 18–19
will of the people 86, 93, 157
"worst sort" narrative 5, 82, 92, 94

Zelensky, Volodymyr 147

www.ingramcontent.com/pod-product-compliance
Lightning Source LLC
Chambersburg PA
CBHW061837300426
44115CB00013B/2418